The OXFORD Children's A to Z of Art

Malcolm and Meryl Doney

OXFORD
UNIVERSITY PRESS

OXFORD
UNIVERSITY PRESS

Great Clarendon Street, Oxford OX2 6DP

Oxford University Press is a department of the University of Oxford. It furthers the University's objective of excellence in research, scholarship, and education by publishing worldwide in

Oxford New York

Auckland Cape Town Dar es Salaam Hong Kong Karachi Kuala Lumpur Madrid Melbourne Mexico City Nairobi New Delhi Shanghai Taipei Toronto

With offices in

Argentina Austria Brazil Chile Czech Republic France Greece Guatemala Hungary Italy Japan Poland Portugal Singapore South Korea Switzerland Thailand Turkey Ukraine Vietnam

Oxford is a registered trade mark of Oxford University Press in the UK and in certain other countries

British Library Cataloguing in Publication Data

Data available

ISBN 978-0-19-911257-9

10 9 8 7 6 5 4

Printed in China

Illustrations

John Bendall-Brunello: 10, 15, 18, 27, 29, 30, 32, 45, 54

Jean-Louis Besson: 4/5

Children's Art

Artworks, Oxford with warmest thanks to the children and their teacher Joanne Acty for lending their work:
p 17t not known; p 22t Emmie van Biervliet; p 34b Simon Timms; p 39b Kate Hobby; p 43t Kate Hobby; p 44cl Oliver Matthews, Mungo Pay, Nathaniel Sherbourne, Jos Spafford-Baker; p 48t James Wilson; p 48 bl Jack Brougham; p 52t Kate Hobby; p 55t Jack Brougham; p 56c Laura Thompson-Lynch; p 57cl Rhiannon Davies; p 58tr Neil Sadler; p 58c not known; p 58bl not known; p 59tr Lucy Parker; p 59cl not known; p 60 Clare Battle; p 61t after Seurat's Bathers at Asnières by Alice Watanabe

Courtesy of Dulwich Picture Gallery Education Department
p 17t graffiti collage interpretation of Jacob van Ruisdael Landscape with Windmills near Haarlem, created by the children of Rosendale Junior School, London: Katie Jackson, Nicola Peacock, Matthew Jellow, Chibeza Agley, Natalie Peach, Fiona Morton, Poppy Beale-Collins, Jason Mabbs

Thea Wright p 55b

Acknowledgements

Design: Sally Boothroyd
Picture research: Suzanne Williams
Abbreviations: t = top; b = bottom; l = left; r = right; c = centre; back = background

Photographs

The publishers would like to thank the following for permission to reproduce the following photographs:

Front cover: tl Van Gogh Sunflowers, 1888, oil on canvas, 92.1 x 73, The National Gallery, London/Corbis

tr textile by Clare Battle

bl Easter Island statue Corbis/Charles & Josette Lenars

br elephant triptych by Emmie van Biervliet

Back cover and spine: tl and tr courtesy of Winsor & Newton
b Melissa Orrom Swan

Inside book: Albright-Knox Art Gallery, Buffalo, New York
p36t Frida Kahlo Self-Portrait with Monkey, 1938, oil on masonite 40.64 x 30.48. Bequest of Conger Goodyear, 1966

The Bridgeman Art Library p9b Louvre, Paris/Lauros-Giraudon; p10 Private Collection, by permission of the artist's estate; p13 Uffizi Gallery, Florence; p14 Offentliche Kunstsammlung, Basle, Switzerland; © ADAGP, Paris and DACS, London, 1998; p15 Musée d'Orsay, Paris/Lauros-Giraudon; p16t Norfolk Castle Museum; © ADAGP, Paris and DACS, London, 1998; p16- 17b Salford Museum and Art Gallery, Lancashire, by permission of the artist's estate; p19tr Musée d'Orsay, Paris; p21tl Barovier Cup c. 1460-70, Museo Vetrario, Murano, Italy; p22b Prado, Madrid; p22c Prado, Madrid/Index; p23 Graphische Sammlung Albertina, Vienna; p29 Rudolph Staechlin Family Foundation, Basle; p30 Musée d'Orsay, Paris; p31 Prado, Madrid/Index; p33 by permission of the artist's estate; p34t British Library, London; p35 British Museum; p37tl Osterreichische Galerie, Vienna; p38 Louvre, Paris; p39t Courtauld Institute Galleries, University of London; p42b Vatican Museums & Art Gallery, Vatican City; p44br Nasjonalgalleriet, Oslo; © The Munch-Museum/ The Munch-Ellingsen Group/ DACS 1998; p45t Private Collection/Agnew's, London, by permission of the artist's estate; p46br Osaka Museum of Fine Arts, Japan; p47br Oriental Museum, Durham University; p49t Museo Nacional Centro de Arte Reina Sofia, Madrid © Succession Picasso/DACS 1998; p52b Prado, Madrid; p53 Musée d'Orsay, Paris/Giraudon; p54t Museo d'Arte Moderno di Ca Pesaro, Venice; p57b Private Collection; p62 b Kunsthistorisches Museum, Vienna

The National Museum, Copenhagen p25b;

Corbis p6t and p7l/Nowlangie Rock, Kakadu National Park, Northern Territories/Penny Tweedie; p6 Richard A.Cooke III/Heye Foundation, New York; p7tr/Charles & Josette Lenars; p8-9t Photo G. Meyer/ Jackson Pollock Number 27, 1950, 124.5 x 269 cm, Whitney Museum of American Art, New York © ARS, NY and DACS, London, 1998; p20b Charles and Josette Lenars; p21c By Permission of the State Hermitage Museum, St Petersburg; p 21br Michael Freeman; p24-25 background image/Caroline Penn; p25cl Kimbell Art Museum, Fort Worth, Texas; p43b Alexander Burkatowski/Pushkin Museum, Moscow; p46t and p47tr Philip de Bay/Historical Picture Archive; p46tc Richard Swiecki/Royal Ontario Museum p47bl Sakamoto Research Laboratories; p49b Private Collection

Corbis/ The National Gallery, London p18t John Constable The Hay Wain, 1821, oil on canvas, 130.2 x 184.5; p 27 Jan van Eyck The Arnolfini Marriage, 1434 oil on oak, 81.8 x 59.7; p28 cr Thomas Gainsborough The Painter's Daughters chasing a Butterfly, c. 1756, oil on canvas, 113.7 x 104.8; p51tr Raphael The Madonna and Child with the Infant Baptist (The Garvagh Madonna) c. 1509-10, oil on wood, 38.7 x 32.7; p54b Henri Rousseau Tiger in a Tropical Storm (Surprised!) 1891, oil on canvas, 129.8 x161.9; p56t Georges-Pierre Seurat Bathers at Asnières, 1884, oil on canvas, 201 x 300; p62t Paolo Uccello The Battle of San Romano c.1450-60, tempera on poplar, 182 x 320

Cordon Art p26 M.C.Escher's 'Relativity' © 1998 Cordon Art B.V.- Baarn – Holland.
All rights reserved. Permission no B.98.169

Corel; p12bl

Dover Books p9t; p23; p50t; p59tl

David Hockney p32 A Large Diver (Paper Pool 27), 1978, coloured pressed paper pulp, 182.88 x 434.34 © David Hockney/Tyler Graphics Ltd;
p48 br The Brooklyn Bridge, November 1982, photographic collage 276.86 x 147.32 © David Hockney

Michael Holford p7br Victoria & Albert Museum, London; p11 Bayeux Museum; p24t; p24bl British Museum; p25t; p46bl;

Museum of Modern Art, New York Andrew Wyeth, Christina's World, 1948. Tempera on gesso panel 82 x 121.29. Purchase. (16.49). By kind permission of the artist.

The Henry Moore Foundation; p 44t

Melissa Orrom Swan p59b

Paul Spooner, Cabaret Mechanical Theatre p36b Photo by Heini Schneebeli

Tate Gallery, London 1998 p12tl Peter Blake, The Toy Shop, 1962, 156.8 H x 194 W x 34 D © Peter Blake, all rights reserved, DACS 1998; p19bl Salvador Dali Lobster Telephone, 1936 17.8 x 33 x 17.8 © Salvador Dali Foundation Gala - Salvador Dali/ DACS 1998; p28bl Dame Elisabeth Frink, Harbinger Bird IV, 1960, bronze 48.3 H x 21.3 W x 35.6 D, by permission of the artist's estate; p37cr Ford Madox Brown The Hayfield, 1855-6, oil on canvas, 24.1 x 33.3; p50b Roy Lichtenstein Whaam!, 1963 acrylic on canvas 172.7 x 406.4 © Estate of Roy Lichtenstein/ DACS 1998; p51 cl John Everett Millais, Ophelia 1851-2, oil on canvas, 76.2 x 111.8; p61b J.M.W.Turner, Norham Castle, Sunrise c.1845-50, oil on canvas 91 x 122; p63 Andy Warhol, Marilyn Diptych, 1962, acrylic on canvas, 410.8 x 289.6 © The Andy Warhol Foundation for the Visual Arts Inc/ ARS, NY and DACS, London 1998

Wedgwood Museum; p 20tc

Courtesy of Winsor & Newton p 40 t, bl, br; p 41 t, b

Dear Reader

Art is everywhere! You can find it on posters, CD covers, book jackets, T-shirts, and in galleries and museums. As long as there have been human beings on this planet, there has been art.

People make art for many reasons. Some do it as a way of helping them remember important people or events, others because of their religious beliefs. People have made art to protest against governments, or express an opinion. Some artists want to shock people, whereas some just want to show how beautiful the world is.

And because every artist - like every person - is an individual, no one piece of hand-made art is ever the same as another. It's an original which tells us something about the person who made it, and the time and the country he or she comes from.

In this book we want to show you some of the images and objects made by people from all over the world, in different times. We will also introduce you to some of the fascinating people who made them. You won't like some of the things and you may not always understand them - sometimes even the artists can't explain what they're doing! But we do hope you will want to start exploring the exciting and mysterious world of art for yourself.

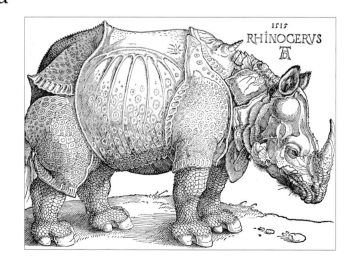

Malcolm & Meryl Doney.

Timeline

BC 30000-3000 Prehistoric world

BC 3200-332 Egyptian Empire, Africa

BC 2500-1750 Indus Valley civilization, India

BC 2300-1400 Minoan civilization, Crete

BC 2000-1400 Stonehenge, Celtic Britain

BC 1600-1100 Mycenaean civilization, Greece

BC 1480-1050 Shang Dynasty, China

BC 1200-300 Olmec Indians, Mexico

BC 1000-1150 AD Celtic Empire, Europe

BC 1100-300 Ancient Greek Empire, Greece

BC 605 Birth of Lao-tzu, founder of Taoism

BC 560 Birth of Buddha, Prince Siddhartha Gautama

1368-1644 Ming Dynasty, China

1526-1676 Mogul Empire, India

1600-1700 Classicism: Poussin

1600s Caravaggio, Rembrandt, Flemish school

1600-1750 Baroque: Rubens

1603-1868 Shogun era, Japan

1690-1750 Rococo: Watteau, Fragonard

1700s Canaletto, Hogarth

1750-1860 Neo-Classicism: David, Ingres

1800s Romanticism: Blake, Géricault, Delacroix, Friedrich

1848 Pre-Raphaelites

1860 Impressionism: Manet, Monet, Renoir

1880 Pointillism: Seurat

1880 Post Impressionism: Cézanne, Van Gogh

Late 1800s Barbizon, Courbet, Constable, Turner

1885-1910 Symbolism

1890-1910 Art Nouveau: Klimt

1905 Fauvism: Matisse

1906 Expressionism: Nolde, Munch

BC 551 Birth of Confucius

BC 500-200 AD Nok culture, Nigeria

BC 450-200 AD La Tène culture, Celtic

BC 30-395 AD Roman Empire

4 AD Birth of Christ

100-1000 AD Axum Dynasty, Ethiopia

300-600 AD Mayan civilization, Central America

320-535 AD Gupta Empire, India

476-1400 AD Byzantine Empire

571 Birth of Mohammed

750-987 Carolingian Empire, France

802-1180 Angkor Empire, Cambodia

850 Russian Empire, Northern Europe

1300-1519 Aztecs, Mexico

1300-1600 Renaissance: (Italy) Donatello, Botticelli, Raphael, Titian, Michelangelo, Leonardo (N. Europe) Dürer, Brueghel

1000-1100 Romanesque age, Europe

1000-1598 Age of the Samurai, Japan

1100-1250 Middle Ages, Europe

1120-1450 Great Zimbabwe, Africa

1140-1550 Gothic age, Europe

1200-1532 Incas, South America

1907 Cubism: Picasso, Braque

Early 1900s Futurism

1913 Vorticism

1914 Dada: Schwitters, Duchamp

1913 Constructivism: Tatlin

1920 Bloomsbury Group

1920-30 Surrealism: Dali, De Chirico

1940-60 Abstract Expressionism: Pollock, De Kooning

1960 Pop Art: Warhol, Lichtenstein

1960 Op Art

1960 Performance Art

1970 Conceptual Art

5

Aboriginal art

The world's most ancient works of art date from around 30,000 BC. This period is called 'prehistoric' because the art of writing had not been developed. We know very little about these peoples, apart from the things that they used and pictures they made.

Body painting was probably the most ancient form of art, but sculptures in clay, bone, stone, wood and ivory were also made. Pottery making and decorating began in the Neolithic period around 6500 BC and the different styles are often used to date the people who made them.

Soon people began to build houses and to make large monuments from huge standing stones, such as Stonehenge in Britain. Another important step was the use of bronze to make all kinds of items ranging from domestic pots, jewellery, and weapons to great sculptures of the gods.

the Americas

People were living in North and South America as early as 30,000 years ago. There are many examples of the paintings they made in caves and on rocks, like the strange figures called the 'Holy Ghost Panel' in Barrier Canyon, Utah.

The native peoples of North America settled on the continent around 4000 BC. They were hunters who used spears and arrowheads made from flint. Later they became the great Native American tribes. The earliest of these were the Hopewell Indians, who made huge animal-shaped mounds like the Great Serpent Mound in Ohio, and the Hohokam Indians, who were known for their colourful pots. The Native Americans also painted animal skins, made baskets and wove textiles. The peoples of the north-west coast made tall, sculpted totem poles. The Inuit peoples of the frozen north carved bone, driftwood, and ivory into miniature Arctic animals.

Africa

Many scientists believe that the first people came from Africa. Paintings dating from around 6000 BC have been found in caves in the Sahara. They show hunters with animals that are now extinct in the area such as the hippopotamus and buffalo. The San (Bushman) rock art of South Africa and Namibia may be even older.

This Native American mask made by the Kwakiutl people is actually two masks. The first face opens to reveal the second.

Australasia

Ancient rock paintings have been found along the Glenelg River in south-east Australia and also in the north-west. The most famous of these shows a man with a halo carrying a kangaroo. **Abstract** paintings (paintings that do not show people, animals or objects) have also been found in central Australia, and this abstract tradition is still maintained by Australian Aboriginal people today.

The native peoples of the islands in Melanesia and Polynesia made highly decorated artefacts, often influenced by art from Asia and the Far East. The mysterious rock statues of Rapa Nui (Easter Island) were made from around AD 1000 onwards.

◁
No one knows who made these magnificent Easter Island heads which look out over the sea.

△ *This striking aboriginal rock painting is in Kakadu National Park in the New Territories of Australia.*

the Far East

China's earliest peoples made painted pottery. The Shang and Zhou dynasties are particularly known for very sophisticated bronze bowls and pots. Objects made from carved jade were also highly prized.

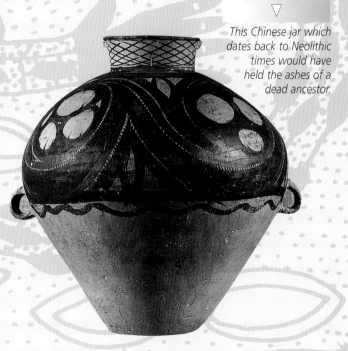

▽
This Chinese jar which dates back to Neolithic times would have held the ashes of a dead ancestor.

A

abstract art

Abstract art is a picture or a sculpture made up of colours and **shapes**. Any pattern or decoration could be described as abstract, but the name 'abstract art' has also come to mean a certain kind of work that artists only started to produce in the 20th century.

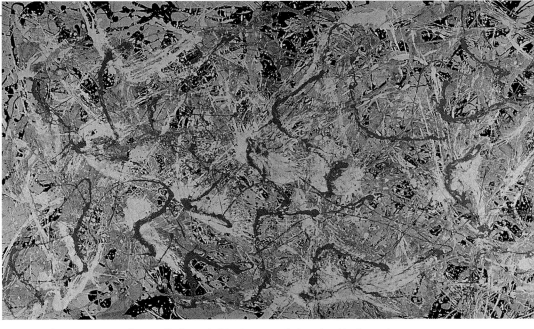

△ Number 27, 1950. Jackson Pollock made his abstract paintings by dripping paint onto the canvas from above. The technique was sometimes called 'action painting'.

There are three main types. The first type is when the artist paints something real – such as a forest or a human body – and represents it in shapes and colours. These might give the general idea of what the original is like, but could not be described as a painting of a forest or a person. The second type is when paintings or sculpture are made up of shapes, **forms** or colours, that are not meant to represent anything else. This is sometimes known as 'non-representational' art. The third type is when works of art express something that the artist is feeling, rather than what they can see.

abstract expressionism

This type of art is usually very large paintings done in broad, free brush strokes. It often represents the artist's feelings expressed in a very direct, quick way onto the canvas. The best-known abstract expressionist was the American painter **Jackson Pollock**.

Albers, Josef

(1888-1976)
A German-born artist who moved to America in the 1930s. He was famous for a series of paintings called 'Homage to the Square' where he explored how different colours looked next to one another.

Andre, Carl

(1935-)
Carl Andre is an American sculptor who likes to use materials someone else has produced (such as bricks or concrete blocks) which he places in geometrical **patterns** on the floor. He became infamous in Britain in 1976 when the Tate Gallery bought a piece made of 120 fire bricks laid out in an oblong shape. Some people thought it was a waste of money and not art at all.

Andrea del Sarto

(1486-1530)
Andrea del Sarto lived in Florence, Italy at the same time as Michelangelo and Raphael. He is admired for the huge variety of wonderful colours in his painting. He produced the colours himself by mixing several paints. He was known as 'del Sarto' which means 'the tailor' because that was his father's trade.

Angelico, Fra

(c.1395-1455)
Fra Angelico (Brother Angelico) was a Dominican monk from Florence, Italy. He received commissions which took him all over Italy producing beautiful, calm pictures, usually on **religious** themes.

architecture

Architecture is about the design of buildings. A professional designer of buildings is called an architect. Like almost anything that is **designed** by creative people, buildings in each age and from every culture show the tastes and ideas of their own times.

People have not always lived in buildings. The first humans lived in caves or found shelter wherever they could. It was only when they began to grow crops and needed to stay in one place that they began to make simple buildings.

Often they were huts made out of materials found nearby, such as branches and animal skins over a wooden framework. In some parts of the world people still live in huts whose simple, but effective, designs have not changed for centuries.

Elsewhere people discovered other ways of making grander, more complicated buildings – often in honour of gods or powerful rulers. These include mighty stone buildings such as Angkor Wat in present-day Kampuchea, the ziggurat of Mesopotamia or the Egyptian and Mayan 'pyramids'.

As Christianity became a powerful religion, the best architects and craftsmen were employed to build churches and cathedrals. These too have changed **shape** and **style** over the centuries. In each new age, new materials and new ways of making buildings have changed the shape of our towns and cities. Soaring skyscrapers, cantilevered roofs and enormous glass walls are now possible. However, many people feel more comfortable in older buildings and architects still borrow ideas and styles from the past to use in their latest designs.

 An illustration from a 15th century book on perspective in buildings by Jan Vredeman de Vries.

Arcimboldo, Giuseppe

(1527-93)
Giuseppe Arcimboldo was a painter from Milan, Italy. He became famous for his strange paintings of people made entirely of fruit and vegetables, animals or tools.

 Summer, 1573. Arcimboldo has cleverly created a man's head from a feast of summer fruits.

art school

Art schools, also known as colleges of art, are the art world's version of universities, where people train to become artists or **designers**.

art therapy

Art therapy is a way of using art to help people who are recovering from an illness or suffering from psychological problems. They are encouraged to paint and draw as part of their treatment.

artefact

An artefact is any object or thing – it could be a bowl or a tool or a painting – that is made by people.

artist

An artist is a person who makes art.

avant-garde

Avant-garde is a French military term for the soldiers fighting at the front of a battle. It has now come to mean artists who are doing a dramatically new or different type of work compared to those before them. They are on the 'front line' of art.

Bacon, Francis

(1909-92)

Francis Bacon was born in Dublin, Ireland. He did not go to art school, but rose to become one of Britain's most important painters. His pictures are not pleasant to look at, but they are extremely powerful images. He often shows a single person who appears lost, lonely and sometimes terrified. Bacon uses swipes of paint to smudge and twist their faces and bodies into characters from a nightmare.

△ Pope No. 2, 1960. Francis Bacon painted a series of pictures of Popes. This one includes an animal carcass.

Baroque

The word 'Baroque' began as an insult, meaning absurd or grotesque. It was used by critics in the 19th century to describe European art of the 17th century which they thought was too fancy. Baroque is still used to describe the very 'busy' style of the period.

 This section of the Bayeux Tapestry shows horsemen being killed during the Battle of Hastings.

Baselitz, Georg

(1938-)

Georg Baselitz is a German-born painter who, since 1969, has painted his expressionistic people upside down so that at first sight they look like shapes and colours. He also makes wooden sculptures of roughly hacked out human figures.

Basquiat, Jean-Michel

(1960-86)

Jean-Michel Basquiat was a New York street artist who began by making illegal paintings of street life on the city's subway. He was soon discovered by the international art world and became a huge success. He died from a drugs overdose at the age of 26.

Bauhaus

The Bauhaus was a school of art and **design** founded by the German architect Walter Gropius in Weimar in 1909. It helped to start a revolution in building and furniture design by combining creative ideas and new methods of making things in materials such as steel and glass. The school became known for its severe, undecorated designs. In a very short time it grew to become the most famous art school of the century, before it was closed by the Nazis in 1933.

Bayeux Tapestry

The Bayeux Tapestry was made around the year 1080 – shortly after the Battle of Hastings. It uses detailed embroidery to tell the story of the battle, rather like a strip **cartoon**. Very little medieval art of its kind has survived because tapestries and hangings hung in castles that were destroyed in war.

the Bellini family

The Bellinis were a talented family of painters who lived in Venice, Italy in the 15th and 16th centuries. Jacopo (c.1400-70) was the father who was also father-in-law to the well-known Italian painter Mantegna. He had two sons, Gentile (1429-1507) and Giovanni (c.1430-1516). Both were taught by their father and became great artists. Giovanni, the younger son, was the most successful, and because of him Venice became almost as important in the art world as Florence and Rome.

Bernini, Gianlorenzo

(1598-1680)

Bernini was the best-known Italian artist of the **Baroque** style. An intensely religious man, his faith showed in his work. He was a painter, sculptor, **architect** and **designer** who could turn his hand to anything. In 1665 he put on an opera in Rome where he composed the music, wrote the words, painted the scenery, made the sculptures and invented the stage machinery – all in a building which he had designed!

Beuys, Josef

(1921-86)

Josef Beuys was a German sculptor and **performance** artist. As a Luftwaffe pilot in 1943 he had been shot down and was rescued by Tartar nomads who covered his wounded body in fat and wrapped it in felt. When he became an artist in his 40s, Beuys used these materials in his work as symbols of healing.

 The Toy Shop, 1962. Peter Blake has recreated a 1950s shop front, using some of his own collection of cheap toys.

Blake, Peter

(1932-)

Peter Blake is a British painter in the **pop art** tradition. His best-known piece is the cover of the Beatles' album, 'Sergeant Pepper's Lonely Hearts Club Band'. His work is witty and full of nostalgic references to a Britain of the past.

Blake, William

(1757-1827)

William Blake was a British artist, philosopher and poet. He tried to portray the spiritual world which he thought was beyond the one we can see. He trained as an engraver and in 1787 developed a new method of **printing** which he believed had been revealed to him by his dead brother. He used this method to illustrate his own collections of poems such as 'Songs of Innocence'.

Bloomsbury Group

The Bloomsbury Group was a collection of writers and artists in London, England, during the 1920s and 30s. The group turned its back on Victorian ideas and welcomed a more modern outlook. They included Clive and Vanessa Bell, the novelist Virginia Woolf, Lytton Strachey, Roger Fry, Dora Carrington and Duncan Grant. They took the name Bloomsbury from the area of London where the Bells lived and the group often met.

body art

In body art, artists use their own bodies for their work. They may video or photograph themselves, or perform in public. It is similar to **conceptual** and **performance art**.

This Karawari woman from New Guinea is using body art to show her village colours.

Bonnard, Pierre

(1867-1947)

Pierre Bonnard was a French painter who loved to paint scenes from domestic life. He used glowing, sunlit colours, especially after he moved south to the hot Mediterranean coast at Cannes. His favourite model was his wife Marie, whom he often painted in the bath because she had an obsession with washing.

Bosch, Hieronymus

(c.1450-1516)

Hieronymus Bosch was a Dutch painter who is best known for his fantastic scenes of heaven and hell, full of strange half-human, half-animal creatures and demons. Very little is known about him except that his paintings are obsessed with showing evil and temptation.

Botticelli, Sandro

(1445-1510)

Sandro Botticelli was an Italian painter from Florence who is now one of the most popular painters of the period known as the **quattrocento** (15th century). His figures are very graceful, drawn with flowing lines. There is something delicate, almost feminine about Botticelli's work, which in later years influenced Art Nouveau and the members of the **Pre-Raphaelite Brotherhood.**

Boudin, Eugène

(1824-98)

Eugène Boudin was a French painter, best known for his beach scenes and **seascapes** of northern France where he lived. These pictures, painted on the spot, could just as easily be called sky-scapes, since the sky often takes up two-thirds of the **space**.

Brancusi, Constantin

(1876-1957)

Constantin Brancusi was a Romanian sculptor who came to Paris to work. He was introduced to the sculptor **Rodin** who invited him to be his assistant but he refused the offer, saying, 'No other trees can grow in the shadow of an oak'. Brancusi particularly loved simple, smooth egg-like **forms** which he believed were at the heart of nature.

▽ *The Birth of Venus, c.1485. Botticelli's picture of this ancient Greek story is one of his best-known paintings.*

Still Life with a Violin and a Pitcher, 1910. Braque gives the jug and the violin a cubist treatment, breaking up the objects into fragments.

Braque, Georges

(1882-1963)
Georges Braque was a leading French **cubist** painter working in Paris at the same time as **Picasso**. In fact Braque and Picasso could be called the inventors of **cubism**. Braque concentrated on painting arrangements of objects in his studio – a violin, a newspaper, a vase, a bowl of fruit – using a **collage** of paper, wood and fabric as well as paint.

Brueghel, Pieter (the elder)

(c.1525-69)
Pieter Brueghel was a Flemish painter who painted peasant life, teeming with people and everyday activity. In the years after the Reformation it was difficult for painters to make a living, since **religious** pictures were not encouraged. Flemish artists like Brueghel were able to survive because they had always painted scenes from everyday life. Brueghel's two sons, Jan and Pieter the younger, were also successful painters.

Byzantine art

Byzantine art is work produced during the period of the Eastern Roman Empire, founded by the first Christian Emperor Constantine in AD 330. Its influence lasted until 1453, when the capital city, Constantinople (originally called Byzantium), was captured by the Turks. Most typical of Byzantine art are the wonderful **mosaics** of **religious** scenes to be found in Byzantine churches.

C

Calder, Alexander

(1898-1976)
Alexander Calder was an American sculptor and painter who invented the **mobile** and was one of the pioneers of **kinetic art**. As a young man he studied mechanical engineering and his carefully-balanced constructions – often made of wire and flat metal **shapes** – were sometimes hung from the ceiling so that they moved in the air.

camera obscura

A camera obscura (Latin words that mean 'dark chamber') is a piece of apparatus that works like a camera to project the image of an object or a whole scene onto a sheet of paper or ground glass.

Canaletto

(1697-1768)
Canaletto was a Venetian painter famous for his picturesque views of Venice. He often used the **camera obscura** to help him at an early stage of **composing** his pictures.

Caravaggio, Michelangelo Merisi da

(1571-1610)
The Italian painter Caravaggio was very controversial in his day because he painted powerful scenes from the Bible as if they were happening in his own time instead of long ago. He thought it was very important to make the events in his painting look real, not posed. His wild behaviour in his personal life also caused scandals. For example, he once had to run away from Rome after he had used a dagger to kill a man, all over a bet they had on a tennis match!

Caro, Anthony

(1924-)
Anthony Caro is a British sculptor who is best known for his huge **abstract** pieces made out of girders and sheet metal, welded together and painted in one colour. More recently he has returned to making sculptures out of bronze.

cartoon

The word cartoon has two meanings. Nowadays it means a funny drawing or animated story, but originally a cartoon was the full-size drawing that an artist would make before starting on a painting.

carving

To carve something means to cut it out of something solid. So a statue might be carved out of wood using knives and chisels. An object, such as a statue, which has been carved is sometimes called a carving.

Cassatt, Mary

(1844-1926)
Mary Cassatt was an American painter who showed her work with the French **impressionists**. She specialized in painting tender scenes of everyday life.

Cézanne, Paul

1839-1906)
Paul Cézanne was a French painter who exhibited with the **impressionists** but soon developed a different style. He moved to the South of France and spent his working life painting from nature, often painting the same scene over and over again. In his work he was trying to understand the **patterns** and **shapes** at the heart of nature. He did not try to make the **drawing** or the colour 'correct', but was prepared to distort them to fit the overall **design** of his pictures. His willingness to question what he could see made Cézanne a major influence on other 20th century artists – especially the **cubists**.

▽ *Apples and Oranges, 1895-1900. A beautiful example of one of Cézanne's many still lifes.*

Chagall, Marc

(1887-1985)

Marc Chagall was a Russian-born painter who worked most of his life in France. His paintings seem like fairy tales or dreams – full of wonder and energy. Chagall said that all his pictures were based on memories of his early life in Russia.

chiaroscuro

Chiaroscuro is an Italian word used to describe the effects of light and dark in a picture.

Chirico, Giorgio de

(1888-1978)

Giorgio de Chirico was born in Greece but painted mostly in Italy. His best-known paintings were of eerie, empty squares where statues or tailors' dummies stood in the late afternoon sun, casting long shadows. These silent, dreamlike pictures, with their odd **perspective**, were a big influence on the **surrealist** movement.

Christo Javacheff

(1935-)

Christo Javacheff is a sculptor who was born in Bulgaria, but is now an American citizen. He calls his art 'empaquetage' (packaging). He started by wrapping materials around small objects such as paint tins, but soon became more ambitious. Among other things, he has wrapped a section of coastline, a bridge over the River Seine in Paris and the entire Reichstag parliament building in Germany.

cityscape

A cityscape is a painting of city buildings, usually a broad view over the rooftops to the horizon.

The Artist in his Studio, c. 1930. Chagall is in his studio surrounded by his memories.

Claude Lorraine

(1600-82)

Often known simply as Claude, this painter was born in Lorraine in France (which is where his surname came from). He worked mostly in Italy, painting **landscapes** of the countryside around Rome, which he used as a backdrop for classical and biblical stories. These were bathed in light and people found them so beautiful that they would try to find Claude-type countryside for their picnics. British garden **designers** used them as inspiration for their work.

Coming from the Mill, 1930. L. S. Lowry became Britain's most popular painter of cityscapes.

collage

A collage is a picture made by sticking all sorts of different materials such as newspaper, ceramics, objects, photographs or textiles onto a surface.

The artist can use colour in a painting to try to imitate what he or she can see. But artists also use colours to express feelings and moods. For instance, shades of red create a warm feeling, while shades of blue create a cooler effect.

Some artists have spent many years experimenting with colour to see what happens when you put different combinations close to one another. You might try to see what happens when you put a block of bright red next to its complementary green. Watch out for the buzz!

composition

The composition of a painting is the art of placing all the different items (such as a tree, a person and a building) so that the final picture looks well balanced.

conceptual art

Conceptual art is work where the most important thing is the thought or the idea that the artist has. Conceptual artists often simply produce writings or documents to explain their ideas and show these as the art itself.

Collage made by the children of Rossendale Junior School, based on a painting by the Dutch artist Jacob van Ruisdael.

colour

The colours that artists use are made up of the primary colours (red, blue and yellow). With these three, plus black and white, you can make up almost any colour you like. Red and yellow make orange, for example, and yellow and blue make green. Mix all three together and you get brown. Each of the primary colours has a kind of opposite, called a complementary colour. Complementaries are made up of the other two primary colours. For example, the complementary colour to blue is orange (made by mixing yellow and red). All these colours can be made a lighter shade by mixing in white, or a darker shade by mixing in black.

This painting in acrylic shows a bold use of colour. Child artist (unknown).

Constable, John

(1776-1837)

Constable was a British **landscape** painter who wanted to paint a true image of the country-side he saw around him, particularly the scenery in Suffolk where he was born. He saw that the landscape changed with the different light, weather conditions and seasons. He tried to catch the freshness of these effects by **drawing** and making oil **sketches** outside before producing the finished paintings in his studio.

The Hay Wain, 1821. Constable's picture of a hay wagon in a mill pond shows how the artist was interested in the beauties of the Suffolk countryside.

Courbet, Gustave

(1819-77)

Courbet was a French painter dedicated to what he called 'realism'. He hated posed figures and romantic, un-real **landscapes**. He wanted his landscapes to look natural. Some **critics** thought his work ugly. Once, when he was making a painting for a church, someone asked him to include an angel. He replied, 'Show me an angel and I will paint one'.

critic

An art critic is someone who writes about the work that artists do, and the exhibitions at which various kinds of art are shown.

cubism

Cubism was an important 20th century art movement, started by the French painters **Picasso** and **Braque**. It began around 1907 when these two, and other artists who followed them, broke away from the idea that art copied what you could see from a single point of view. They believed that we recognize an object because we can see it from all sides. In their paintings, they broke up the **shapes** of objects and people, so that we could see several sides at once.

They experimented with **collage**, using pieces from newspapers and strips of material. Their pictures were completely different from anything that artists before them had produced.

This dramatically new way of seeing things, and of making art, revolutionized the art world. Although cubism was never **abstract** – traces of real objects could always be seen in these pictures – it opened up the possibility that art might not contain any recognizable objects at all.

D

Dada

Dada was an art movement that grew up in Zurich, Switzerland, shortly after the First World War. No-one is sure where the name came from and it may have been chosen at random. Because Switzerland was a neutral country, a number of artists from all over Europe had taken shelter there. Partly as a reaction to the horror of the war, these artists decided that they wanted to forget the art of the past and to make shocking new art that was playful and allowed things to happen by accident. There was no fixed Dada style, it was more of an attitude of mind. As the movement grew, other groups started in Berlin and New York. Two of the best-known Dada artists are **Kurt Schwitters** and **Marcel Duchamp**.

Dali, Salvador

(1904-89)

Salvador Dali was a Spanish painter who became part of the **surrealist** movement which was interested in dreams and the unconscious mind. He became famous for his smoothly-painted pictures featuring burning giraffes and melting watches. He once called his pictures 'hand-painted dream photographs'.

Lobster Telephone, 1936. Surrealists like Salvador Dali enjoyed making visual jokes such as this.

David, Jacques Louis

(1748-1825)

David was a Frenchman who painted heroic scenes of the French Revolution in the style of the ancient Greeks and Romans. His uncluttered style of painting was a reaction against the 'fussiness' of artists before him.

Davis, Stuart

(1894-1964)

Davis was an American painter and pioneer of **pop art**. First he was influenced by **cubism**; later he introduced bright colours and bold lettering from US advertisements and posters. In the 1920s–40s he produced vivid paintings reflecting fast city life and jazz.

△ *Dancers in Blue, c.1890. Edgar Degas.*

Degas, Edgar

(1834-1917)

Degas was a French painter and sculptor, best known for his paintings and **drawings** of ballet dancers, which look completely spontaneous – as if the artist had painted them in the theatre. The figures are often cut off by the edge of a picture, an idea that Degas borrowed from photographs and Japanese **prints**.

De Kooning, Willem

(1904-97)

De Kooning was a Dutch-born painter who travelled to America as a stowaway on board a ship. He was a leading **abstract expressionist**, and his most powerful works are his energetic pictures of fierce, distorted women.

The decorative arts

As long as people have been making useful objects – from pottery bowls to chairs – they have tried to make them beautiful as well as practical. They have used **design** and colour and **shape**, just as visual artists do. This use of art is often called the decorative arts.

pottery

Pottery is a good example. People have made pottery objects for thousands of years. At first they made them from clay and dried them in the sun – like bricks. Later they discovered that if they were baked at a higher temperature then the clay became harder, stronger and smoother. Potters developed a special oven called a kiln to bake or 'fire' their pots.

Anything made from pottery is also called ceramic, which comes from the ancient Greek word for potter's clay, 'keramos'. Ceramics are often decorated with pictures or patterns in different coloured glazes which, when they are fired in the kiln, fuse on to the pottery base.

There are three basic types of pottery:
Earthenware – the crudest form of pottery – fired at low temperatures.
Stoneware – harder and smoother – fired at medium temperatures.
Porcelain – the finest and smoothest of all – fired at very high temperatures.

The making of fine porcelain was invented by the Chinese which is why cups and saucers are sometimes called china. For hundreds of years the Chinese, and later the Japanese, kept the process a secret. Europeans did not learn to make porcelain until the 1700s. Soon factories were set up and talented artists were employed to make and decorate porcelain figures and pots. Probably the most famous European producers of fine porcelain in the eighteenth century were the Meissen factory in Germany and Josiah Wedgwood in Britain.

A porcelain teapot designed by Josiah Wedgwood.

textiles

People have woven textiles for at least 11,000 years. They found they could colour thread or yarn with dyes made from insects or plants and produce multicoloured or patterned fabrics for clothes or for use in the home. People have also embroidered textiles with **patterns** or pictures from the very earliest days.

Different countries or areas have become known for different kinds of weaving. For instance, China and Persia were famous for their beautiful carpets and Northern Europe for its tapestries (woven pictures that were hung on the wall).

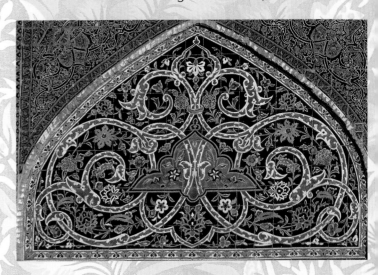

Delicate mosaic wall decoration from the Kazimayan Mosque, Baghdad, Iraq.

glass

Glassmaking is a more recent decorative art – the process is about 3,500 years old. Glass is made when you melt sand in a furnace: once it is hot enough it turns into a clear liquid. When it was first invented, molten glass was either poured into a mould or blown into a shape. Different materials were added to change the colour or to improve its transparency. While the glass is still warm and soft it can be worked into different shapes and designs. Once the glass has cooled and become hard it can be decorated by engraving, etching or sandblasting.

△ *15th century Italian marriage cup with portraits of the bride and groom.*

The Romans made fine glass but the best-known craftsmen were the Venetians, who made thin, beautiful glassware known as Cristallo. In the 1500s the English developed an even clearer, heavier glass called lead crystal whose surface could be cut into patterns.

▷ *Highly decorated piece of 19th century German jewellery.*

metal

Gold and silver are soft metals and easy to work with – they are also rare and expensive. As a result, gold and silver jewellery have always been symbols of wealth and rank. Talented goldsmiths and silversmiths in every age have earned great respect for their skills. Those working with less precious metals are less highly thought of, but the elegant work in wrought iron for such things as balconies and gates is an art in itself.

furniture

Since most furniture has been made of wood, which does not last very well, it is difficult to know what early furniture looked like. What has been preserved tells us that people used the same sort of things we do now – chairs, tables, cupboards and boxes. Over the years, techniques for making furniture have improved, but from the earliest times, woodworkers have carved and decorated furniture with **patterns** and symbols. Cabinet-makers used lathes to make the shapes rounder or used heat to bend it into shapes. They also used different kinds of wood to make intricate patterns.

The 1700s is thought to be the greatest time for hand-made furniture. Charles Cressant, cabinet-maker to the French regent Philippe d'Orléans, developed a style known as régence using floral and animal designs. After this came the rococo style made famous by Thomas Chippendale, who was influenced by Chinese designs.

During the 1800s furniture became heavier and darker until the turn of the century when designers began to look for cleaner lines. As technology advanced, furniture could be made more simply and new materials such as metal, plastic and foam rubber were used. Design schools like the **Bauhaus** in Germany promoted geometric designs without decoration. This has been the main influence on furniture in the 20th century.

Nowadays, all these influences are still around and there is no one style that could be called today's form of furniture. The same is true of all the decorative arts. People furnish and decorate their homes according to personal taste – often with a mixture of styles and periods.

▷ *Whistling kettle and plastic salt and pepper set from the 1950s.*

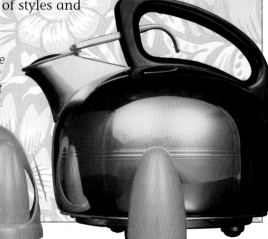

Delacroix, Eugène

(1798-1863)
Delacroix was a passionate French painter who believed that colour was more important than **drawing**, and imagination more important than knowledge. His paintings were full of life and action, perhaps because he painted so quickly. Over 9,000 paintings and drawings were found in his studio after his death.

Delaunay, Robert

(1885-1941)
Robert Delaunay was a French painter who worked alongside the **cubists**. He was especially interested in colour and the sense of movement and flight. His work become more **abstract** as he grew older, featuring circles and target shapes, and his favourite symbol, the Eiffel Tower.

Derain, André

(1880-1954)
André Derain was a French painter who caused a stir when his hot, brightly coloured paintings first appeared. He was one of the creators of **fauvism**.

design

A design is a plan, perhaps in the form of a detailed drawing or a sketch, to show what a finished piece of work ought to look like. This could be the design for a car, a magazine, a house or anything that needs to be made. The **style** or **shape** of the finished thing is also called its design. A **pattern** or decoration on the surface of something (on a tablecloth, for instance) is often called a design.

detail

A detail from a painting or any other piece of art is a small section picked out from the whole picture.

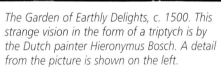

Elephant triptych by Emmie van Biervliet aged 12.

diptych, triptych, polyptych

These are all works of art made up of two or more panels, attached together. A diptych is made from two panels, a triptych from three panels and a polyptych is made from several or many panels.

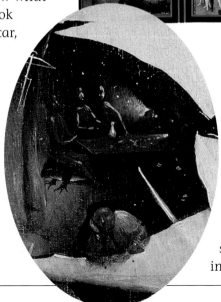

The Garden of Earthly Delights, c. 1500. This strange vision in the form of a triptych is by the Dutch painter Hieronymus Bosch. A detail from the picture is shown on the left.

Donatello

(1386-1466)
Donatello was an Italian sculptor – probably the finest European sculptor of the 15th century. His work shows that he studied the human body very closely, and also showed real human emotions in the images that he created.

drawing

Drawing is very important to all artists. Some use it to improve their skills, just as sportsmen and sportswomen use training sessions. Drawing is useful for trying things out, for taking down visual notes on the spot, or for practising something difficult. Some artists like to draw from objects and people around them, others prefer to draw what they can imagine inside their heads.

Artists draw with many different materials depending on the kind of line they want, the subject they are drawing, or simply how they feel. Charcoal, soft pencils and pen and ink are the most popular drawing materials, but felt tips and pastels can also be used. See special feature on **materials**.

Many artists feel more relaxed when they draw than when they are doing a final painting or making a piece of sculpture. As a result, **sketches** and drawings can reveal an interesting and different side to their work.

Dubuffet, Jean

(1901-85)
Dubuffet was a French painter who developed what he called 'Art Brut' (raw art) influenced by the pictures made by young children and psychiatric patients. These images were often scratched into the surface of the paintings, liked scrawled graffiti.

Duchamp, Marcel

(1887-1968)
Marcel Duchamp helped revolutionize the way we look at art. He was born in France but became part of the **Dada** movement in New York. He tried to break away from tradition by saying that whatever an artist does is a work of art. He placed what he called 'ready mades' in exhibitions, the most famous of which was a urinal which he titled 'Fountain'. His idea backfired, because his 'ready mades' became famous and people were ready to spend a great deal of money to buy them. In his later years, Duchamp gave up making art and simply played chess.

Dufy, Raoul

(1877-1953)
Raoul Dufy was a French painter who helped to make modern art popular. His simple paintings, outlined in black and then washed with luminous colours, are admired for being decorative and joyful.

Dürer, Albrecht

(1471-1528)
Dürer is regarded as one of the greatest artists of the **Renaissance**, although he was not Italian. Born in Germany, he travelled all over Europe, soaking up influences wherever he went. He is probably best known for his skilful engravings and woodcuts, although he was an exceptional painter as well.

The Rhinoceros, 1512-15. This skilful and detailed woodcut is a good example of Dürer's talent.

Dyck, Anthony Van

(1599-1641)
Belgian-born Van Dyck became one of Britain's most famous court painters. He studied under **Rubens** and his **portraits** – often very flattering to his sitters – became so popular that King Charles I of England took him on as his court painter and later made him a knight.

The ruins of Machu
▽ Picchu in Peru show
its magnificent location.

We use the word 'civilization' to mean people who lived in an organized group, often with a ruler, a court and a system of laws. Many of the beautiful things made by these people have been discovered and studied by archaeologists. Each group has added to the story of world art, and the things that were made in those far-off days can still be an inspiration to artists today.

the classical civilizations of Greece and Rome

The Minoans (2300-1400 BC) lived on the island of Crete in the Mediterranean and created beautiful pottery and wall paintings. The things that they made are some of the earliest European art to survive until today. They were followed by the Mycenaeans who lived on mainland Greece (1600-1100 BC), and who made precious items in beaten gold, silver and bronze.

The classical civilizations of Greece and Rome followed.

The bronze head of
Aphrodite from the
◁ first or second
century BC, found
in Eastern Turkey.

Early Greek artists based their work on the simple, geometric **patterns** of the Mycenaeans. These developed into the distinctive Greek patterns on vases and pottery. As time passed, Greek **sculpture** became more and more lifelike. They were trying to show human beings at their most beautiful – especially as many of their sculptures showed gods and goddesses.

When the Romans conquered Greece around 140 BC, Greek artists were employed to make sculptures, to build triumphal arches and to carve **reliefs** of Roman victories. They also decorated Roman houses and public buildings with **mosaics** and paintings like those found at Pompeii. Roman art grew directly from these Greek roots, developing a more realistic style.

South America

The oldest New World civilization is believed to be the Olmec Indians in the Gulf of Mexico. They made large sculpted heads. The Maya of central America built pyramid-style temples and palaces, and developed a picture style of writing. The Toltecs built a capital city called Tula, near present-day Mexico City. The Incas of Peru and Chile were known as the Golden People because of their jewellery and sculpture in gold and the Aztec peoples in Mexico prized work in feathers and weaving, and made jewellery such as lip-plugs, earrings, masks and chest ornaments.

Africa

One of the greatest of Africa's early civilizations grew up around the River Nile in Egypt. The Egyptians believed that the dead needed all their earthly goods in the next life, so they made models to be buried with them. The Christian kingdom of Axum in Ethiopia grew rich on trade in ivory. They built many remarkable churches. These were cut directly into the mountains and were decorated with **murals** of scenes from the Bible and elaborate metal crosses.

The people of the Nok culture in Nigeria were expert at iron smelting. Later the Ife and Benin people of West Africa made beautiful brass sculpted heads. Much of Africa's greatest art has been made by unknown artists for use in religious and tribal ceremonies. African **masks**, in particular, inspired many European artists such as **Picasso** and **Modigliani**.

A powerful bronze statue from the Benin people of West Africa.

Water birds being hunted on the River Nile.

Northern Europe

In Britain and Ireland, the Celtic peoples were known for their metalwork, especially their weapons, ornaments and drinking cups. The Celts who converted to Christianity made huge standing stone crosses and richly illuminated manuscripts. In other parts of Northern Europe the art of **icon** painting was developed by the Orthodox Churches especially in Russia. These paintings were made to teach people about their faith. See also **illumination**.

Ancient Celtic bowl, known as the Gundestrup Cauldron, decorated with pictures of warriors and gods.

the Near East

There have been many great civilizations in Mesopotamia, the area around the great rivers Tigris and Euphrates in modern-day Iraq, Iran, and Turkey. The earliest peoples to produce art in this region were the Persians, Sumerians, Akkadians, Babylonians and the Assyrians.

India

There have been four major influences in Indian art: the great Gupta empire of AD 320-535 when Chandragupta united Northern India; Buddhist sculpture and painting which reached a peak around AD 500; the Hindu temple sculpture at Khajuraho; and the painting of the great Mughal Dynasty of Mongol Muslim rulers from 1525 to the 1700s.

the Islamic world

The art of the Muslim religion, Islam, extends over a wide area, from Indonesia in the east to Morocco and Spain in the west. The Qur'an forbids showing images of God, so the emphasis has been on calligraphy and geometric **patterns**. These can be seen on ceramics, textiles, carpets and metalwork as well as on the walls of palaces and mosques.

E

Ensor, James

(1860-1949)

Ensor was a Belgian painter who filled his pictures with strange, scary people (often wearing carnival **masks**), skeletons and other bizarre figures. His most famous work is a huge religious painting entitled 'The Entry of Christ into Brussels'.

Epstein, Jacob

(1880-1959)

Epstein was an American-born sculptor who settled in England. His early work was denounced as obscene and many of his pieces were heavily criticized and even attacked by vandals. Officials placed a brass plaque over the private parts of the angel that he made for the tomb of the writer Oscar Wilde, but in a night raid, a group of poets and artists removed it.

Ernst, Max

(1891-1976)

German-born Max Ernst produced some of the strangest pictures of the 20th century. He liked to put contradictory ideas and images together. For instance, one of his **collages** was called 'Two children are threatened by a nightingale'. Ernst developed the technique of 'frottage', drawing by using rubbings of different textures.

Escher, Maurits Cornelis

(1898-1972)

M. C. Escher was a Dutch **printmaker** who specialized in producing brilliant optical illusions based on mathematical puzzles.

▷ *Relativity, 1953. Escher sets out to confuse the eye with these ascending and descending staircases.*

expressionism

Expressionism is an approach to art where the artist is more interested in communicating his or her emotions and state of mind than in showing the viewer what something looks like. Artists use bold brush strokes and vigorous **lines** or colours to 'express' their feelings. Painters like **El Greco** could be called expressionistic. **Vincent Van Gogh** started the modern form of expressionism and was followed by the **abstract expressionists** in America.

Eyck, Jan Van

(d.1441)

The Flemish painter Jan Van Eyck was one of the first to use the newly invented oil paints (paint had previously been bound together with egg). Van Eyck used the glowing colours and accuracy that oil paints gave to explore his fascination with details. In his life-like paintings, every surface of every jewel and every animal hair is lovingly reproduced.

F

The Marriage of Giovanni Arnolfini and Giovana Cenami, 1434. The artist has written 'Jan Van Eyck was present' on the far wall. The mirror shows the couple and a third person, who may be Van Eyck himself.

Fauvism

Fauve is a French word meaning 'wild beast'. In 1905 a group of artists, including **Matisse** and **Derain**, showed their work together in Paris. Their paintings were so bold and colourful that a critic said the artists were like 'fauves'. So, for a short while, that was how they became known.

figurative art

Figurative art is painting or sculpture where the artist shows people or objects or scenery so that they can be recognized by the viewer. It is often called representational art and is the opposite of **abstract** or non-representational art which does not try to be 'recognizable'.

fine art

Fine art is art, such as painting or **sculpture**, that is made simply to be admired and enjoyed, rather than for any particular use.

Flemish school

Flemish art comes mostly from the old Netherlands, now in Belgium. The best-known Flemish painters were **Jan Van Eyck** and **Pieter Brueghel**.

form

Form usually means a **shape** or the outer shell of something. An **abstract** artist might use forms or shapes in a painting. People's bodies are sometimes called the human form.

Frankenthaler, Helen

(1928-)
Helen Frankenthaler is an American painter who was most active in the 1950s. She was influenced by the **abstract expressionist Jackson Pollock**, but her paintings were more like huge watercolours. She would pour thin paint onto canvas, so that it looked like a series of beautifully coloured stains, often giving the impression of a **landscape**.

fresco

A fresco (from an Italian word meaning 'fresh') is a painting applied directly onto a fresh plaster surface on a wall. Italian artists would mix their colours with the wet plaster so that the painting became part of the wall itself.

Galleries are the best places to see fine art.

Freud, Lucian

(1922-)

Lucian Freud was born in Germany but came to live and work in Britain. The grandson of psychologist Sigmund Freud, he specializes in large-scale **portraits** and **nudes** with what has been described as a brilliant but cold approach. They are often painted close up and can seem disturbingly alive.

Friedrich, Caspar David

(1774-1840)

Caspar David Friedrich was a German romantic painter who wanted to draw out spiritual and religious feelings from his pictures. He would spend a long time in deep contemplation using what he called his 'spiritual eye' before painting his lonely, haunted **landscapes** of misty mountains and seas.

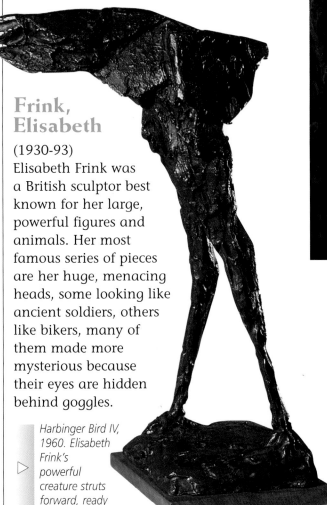

Frink, Elisabeth

(1930-93)

Elisabeth Frink was a British sculptor best known for her large, powerful figures and animals. Her most famous series of pieces are her huge, menacing heads, some looking like ancient soldiers, others like bikers, many of them made more mysterious because their eyes are hidden behind goggles.

▷ Harbinger Bird IV, 1960. Elisabeth Frink's powerful creature struts forward, ready to attack.

Gabo, Naum

(1890-1977)

Naum Gabo was a sculptor who was born in Russia but became an American citizen. He was not trained as an artist, but studied medicine, natural sciences and engineering. He brought these skills to his sculptures which explore the idea of space. He used semi-transparent materials so that the **space** around a sculpture becomes as important as the piece itself.

△ The Painter's Daughters Chasing a Butterfly, c.1759 by Thomas Gainsborough.

Gainsborough, Thomas

(1727-88)

Gainsborough was born in Suffolk, England and taught himself to paint. He became a very successful **portrait** painter with a fresh, individual style and was a friendly rival to the other great British portrait painter of the day, Joshua Reynolds. Gainsborough included **landscape** in his portraits whenever he could.

galleries and museums

In the early years of European art, pictures were painted on the walls of churches and houses, and everyone could enjoy them. Later, pictures were commissioned on board or canvas and kept in the houses of rich families. The ordinary people were unable to see them.

Things changed in the late 1700s when the Royal Academy was founded in England. One of its aims was to put on large exhibitions for the public. After the French Revolution, private collections in France were made public by the new government. The first public art museum was the Louvre in Paris. Eventually museums of art began to open all over Europe. Now almost every major city has a public gallery. Some show art from the past, while others show modern work.

During the 1800s it became fashionable for businessmen to own private collections of art. They would ask other people to find works of art for them and these people became known as art dealers. Many dealers set up galleries (which often started as shops selling artists' materials) where they would show new work. Private galleries still exist – selling art to the public. The dealers earn their money by taking a percentage of the price for each sale.

Gaudier-Brzeska, Henri

(1891-1915)
Gaudier-Brzeska, the French-born sculptor, was killed in World War I at the age of only 23. He was fascinated by primitive sculpture, and produced work that was far ahead of its time.

Gauguin, Paul

(1848-1903)
Paul Gauguin was a French painter who believed that Europe had become too concerned about **style** and longed for a simple, honest life. He left Paris to live on the South Sea Island of Tahiti. Although it was not exactly the paradise he was looking for, he spent two long periods of time there developing paintings with powerful colour and **composition**.

△ *When Are You Getting Married?, 1892. Gauguin fell in love with the tropical island of Tahiti.*

Géricault, Théodore

(1791-1824)
Théodore Géricault was a French painter who loved action-packed pictures – horses and riding in particular. He caused a stir with his vivid painting of a horrific shipwreck 'The Raft of the Medusa'. He died at the age of 33 in a riding accident.

Van Gogh's Bedroom at Arles, 1889. Van Gogh lived in poverty most of his life - this simply furnished room shows how little he owned.

Gogh, Vincent Van

(1853-90)

Vincent Van Gogh is one of the most famous artists who ever lived, yet he only sold one picture in his whole life. Born in Holland, he moved to France to paint, spending his most creative years in Arles, in the warm south. He had severe mental and emotional problems which caused him to slice off his own ear and ended with him taking his own life, but he was extremely thoughtful and thorough about his paintings. Like **Gauguin** and **Cézanne**, he was one of the first few painters to move art away from the need to make pictures look real. Van Gogh's swirling, energetic brush strokes and intense colours revealed at least as much about Van Gogh as they did about the sunflowers or chairs he was painting.

Giorgione, Giorgio

(1477-1510)

There may be only five paintings in existence by the Italian painter Giorgio Giorgione. Yet these few paintings are so different from anything that went before him that they have made his reputation as an important artist. Giorgione was one of the first artists to work for private patrons rather than for public buildings or for the Church. His scenes had a romantic atmosphere about them which was entirely new and had a profound influence on artists like **Titian** and **Giovanni Bellini**.

Giotto di Bondone

(c.1267-1337)

Giotto was an Italian **fresco** painter from Florence who revolutionized the art of painting. Before Giotto, **religious** paintings had been made up of rather flat, stiff arrangements of people. His paintings of Bible stories had more depth in them and viewers could imagine that they were present at the scene of the event.

golden section

The golden section is a measurement of proportion either of a line or of a rectangle, which artists have used for many hundreds of years. It cannot be measured in round numbers, but it is roughly 8:13. It is used in **composing** pictures and for placing important elements within the picture, such as the horizon or the position of a key figure.

Goldsworthy, Andy

(1956-)
Andy Goldsworthy is a British sculptor who works in natural materials such as leaves, rocks or bark – usually making and placing his **sculptures** in the open air. Sometimes his pieces – like those made from icicles – will only last a short time before natural forces make them disappear.

Goncharova, Natalia

(1881-1962)
Natalia Goncharova was a Russian painter and designer who was part of the **avant garde** movement in Moscow. Later she moved to Paris and began to use ideas from Russian folk art and **icons** combined with the influence of French art to make her primitive, almost **abstract** pictures. From 1919 she spent most of her time **designing** theatre sets and costumes.

Gothic

Gothic is the name given to the style of **architecture** in northern Europe from the 12th to the 16th centuries. Gothic churches have pointed arches and tall pillars topped with lacy stonework that looks like tree branches. Art of the same period is also sometimes called Gothic.

Goya, Francisco de

(1746-1828)
Goya was a court painter to the Spanish royal family, but he was also an independent and original artist. His **portraits** make no attempt to flatter his sitters – we can see their faults and vanity. Goya also painted brilliant pictures of his own dark, private visions and nightmares. It is possible that his visions were affected by a mysterious illness which he suffered in his 40s, and which left him deaf.

Greco, El

(1541-1614)
This painter was born on the Greek island of Crete, but settled in Spain. His real name was Theotocopoulos, but he always signed his pictures with his nickname, El Greco, which means 'the Greek' in Spanish. His wild paintings, full of intense religious feeling and distorted, elongated people, look much more modern than they really are.

Guston, Philip

(1913-80)
Philip Guston, the American painter, had three phases to his artistic life. He began as a **mural** artist, painting social and political subjects, and turned to **abstract expressionism** in the 1950s. During the 1960s, when the Vietnam War was raging, he found himself asking why he was going to his studio every day simply 'to adjust a red to a blue'. He returned to **figurative art**, using a strong, almost **cartoon**-like style, to comment on social issues of the day.

Execution of the Defenders of Madrid 3 May 1808, 1814. Goya shows the horror of this scene by placing the lantern in the centre of the picture.

H

Hals, Frans

(1582-1666)

Born in Belgium, Frans Hals moved to Holland where he became a **portrait** painter. He was able to make his pictures look as though they were a kind of snapshot, capturing the moment and the life of the sitter.

Hamilton, Richard

(1922-)

British pop artist Richard Hamilton is best known for a single piece of work. His **collage**, 'Just what is it that makes today's homes so different, so appealing?' was probably the first genuine piece of **pop art**. With its affectionate references to cinema, TV, advertising, magazines and glamour it summed up precisely what pop art was all about.

Hepworth, Barbara

(1903-75)

Barbara Hepworth was a British sculptor famous for her smooth, **abstract** sculptures, often with a hole through the middle. A superb craftswoman, she liked to **carve** her materials directly rather than to cast in metal. She was married to the artist **Ben Nicholson** and they lived as part of a colony of artists in St Ives, Cornwall. She was a friend of the other great British sculptor, **Henry Moore**. She died tragically in a fire at her studio.

Hirst, Damien

(1965-)

Damien Hirst is a British sculptor famous for placing the corpses of animals in tanks of clear chemical liquid. For example, he displayed an entire 14ft-long dead shark which he called 'The Physical Impossibility of Death in the Mind of Someone Living', and also exhibited a cow sliced in half lengthways. Fond of publicity, Hirst is often in the news and art critics are divided about whether he is a great artist or just a clever one.

Hockney, David

(1937-)

David Hockney is Britain's most famous painter, and one of the art world's most colourful personalities. Born in Bradford, he now lives in Los Angeles, California, and much of his work celebrates its sunshine, pastel-painted houses and numerous swimming pools. His paintings are airy, filled with **space** and light and though they may sometimes seem light-hearted, they are painted with a great deal of skill and seriousness.

▽ A Large Diver, Paper Pool 27, 1978. David Hockney has always been fascinated with light on water, particularly in swimming pools.

Hodgkin, Howard

(1932-)
Howard Hodgkin is a British painter known internationally for his use of colour. At first the broad sweeps and splodges of colour seem completely **abstract**, but within the paintings the natural world seems to lurk, partly hidden. There is a suggestion of **landscape** or a room, and each is based on a particular incident such as a dinner party or a visit to a friend.

Hogarth, William

(1697-1764)
William Hogarth was a British painter and engraver who set out to tell moral tales through his work. He painted series of pictures which told a story in several episodes. The most famous of these is 'The Rake's Progress', which charts the tragic story of a young man who went mad after living a wild and irresponsible life.

Hokusai, Katsushika

(1760-1849)
Japanese artist Hokusai was a master of the coloured woodcut. His work was admired by the French **impressionists**, who loved the simple, bold **lines** of the **prints** and the way that artists like Hokusai showed a majestic mountain behind a simple figure performing an everyday task.

Holbein, Hans

(1497-1543)
Holbein was a German painter who came to England after the Reformation when commissions – especially for **religious** pictures – began to dry up. His spectacular talent as a **portrait** painter brought him to the court of Henry VIII. He sometimes included symbols and objects in his portraits to give clues to the sitter's character.

△ *Chop Suey, 1929. Edward Hopper creates a moment of stillness in a city restaurant where sunlight streams through the window onto the table between the two women.*

Hopper, Edward

(1882-1967)
Edward Hopper has become one of America's best-loved painters. His landscapes show his fascination with sunlight and the wide open spaces of the American countryside. He later became known for scenes of city life. People are pictured alone in rooms, or in small groups strangely distanced from one another.

Hunt, William Holman

(1827-1910)
Holman Hunt was a British painter and co-founder of the **Pre-Raphaelite Brotherhood** with **John Everett Millais** and Dante Gabriel Rossetti. His paintings show every detail as accurately as possible. For instance, when he painted the biblical story 'The Scapegoat' he went out to Israel, tethered a goat in the sun and produced the painting on the spot. His most famous painting is 'The Light of the World'.

I

icon

An icon is a picture made to help Christians worship God. Icons are usually paintings of characters from the Bible or of saints, done in a traditional way, using symbols to help thought and prayer.

illumination

Illumination in art is not to do with light, but with decoration. In the Middle Ages monks would illuminate manuscripts – decorating pages from the Bible with beautifully coloured designs and pictures, often using real gold leaf. Later, poems and other kinds of writing were decorated in the same way.

Froissart's Chronicle. An example of late 15th century illumination showing knights at a jousting contest.

illustration

An illustration is a picture that goes with a piece that someone has written, such as a story. It tells the story in pictures. An artist who draws illustrations is known as an illustrator.

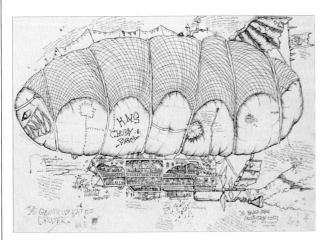
HMS Chubby Piggy. An illustration by Simon Timms (Child artist).

impressionism

Impressionism was one of the most important of all the different movements in art. It began in the 1860s in France, and involved a large number of artists. The best-known are **Cézanne**, **Degas**, **Manet**, **Monet** and **Renoir**. They rejected painting scenes from history or trying to communicate feelings. Instead they tried to record an 'impression' of what their eyes could see at a single moment in time. They were interested in the way that light and colour could be captured and produced bright, fresh pictures with lots of loose brush strokes. This was revolutionary and controversial at the time, and changed the way that people thought about painting.

impressionist

One of the painters belonging to the art movement **impressionism**.

Indian art

The earliest Indian civilizations grew up along the valley of the Indus river at about the same time as the Egyptians and Sumerians. Their cities were decorated with wall reliefs and clay figures of gods.

Hinduism was the first known religion of India, but Buddhism became the greatest influence on Indian art. Buddhist burial mounds, or *stupas*, were built of brick. Small temples of wood were later replaced with greater buildings of brick and stone, decorated with sculptures. In the fourth century the great Gupta Dynasty was founded and Hinduism returned to popularity. Skilled craftsmen and artists made many images of the Hindu gods such as Brahma, Vishnu and Siva. The religion of Islam came to India when invaders from Iran overthrew the last Hindu King of Delhi. They founded the great Mogul Empire. This period

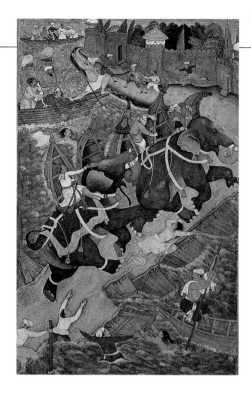

Akbar Tames the Savage Elephant, Haw'i, Outside the Red Fort at Agra, 1590. An action-packed Indian miniature which tells the story of a well-known legend.

was known for its beautiful palaces and buildings such as the Taj Mahal. Calligraphy (beautiful writing) and **miniature** paintings from this period show the Islamic emphasis on **pattern** and **design**.

Islamic art

The earliest followers of Islam worshipped in mosques – simple buildings with a *minbar* or pulpit on the outside from which the people could hear the prophet speak. The Qur'an (Islam's holy book) does not allow artists to represent people, so from the earliest time Muslim artists based their **designs** on geometry, flowers, leaves and Arabic writing repeated in complicated patterns. At first, these designs were used on clay tiles, carved wood and painted stone. Over time, mosque buildings became more and more beautiful with decorated tiles on the walls, courtyards with flower gardens and pools of cool water.

Islamic artists wrote out the words of the Qur'an using many colours, often **illuminated** with gold leaf. Later in Persia and India, pictures were added to illustrate the words. These were copied and the art of **miniature** painting developed. Islamic artists are famous for bowls and dishes in silver, bronze and brass and for luxurious **patterned** carpets.

John, Augustus

(1878-1961)
Augustus John was a British painter and one of the most colourful characters of the British art scene. He was a shy young man who painted methodical pictures until he injured his head diving into the sea on holiday. After this incident he became a rebellious, bohemian 'artist' whose work was energetic, bold and expressive. The rich and famous queued up to have him paint their **portraits.**

John, Gwen

(1876-1939)
Gwen John was Augustus's older sister and his complete opposite. She was a quiet, reclusive character who painted beautiful sad pictures of single figures – usually women. She lived most of her life in France and at one time was the model and companion of the sculptor **Rodin.** She lived in the shadow of her younger brother, but today most people think that she was the better painter.

Johns, Jasper

(1930-)
Jasper Johns is a living American painter. Like a pop artist, Johns uses recognizable things, such as flags, maps and targets, but he paints them in a way that emphasizes the fact that they are painted objects not everyday things. See also **pop art.**

Jones, Allen

(1937-)
Allen Jones is a living British pop artist who first became well known for his slick paintings of women's legs. They were influenced by the illustrations from glamour magazines. Later he made a controversial series of sculptures of women, dressed in rubber clothes, kneeling on all fours with a glass table top on their backs so that they looked like tables. Many **critics** – especially women – thought he was wrong to show women as objects in this way. See also **pop art.**

Kahlo, Frida

(1907-54)
Frida Kahlo was born in Mexico. She had planned to be a doctor but a road accident left her with terrible injuries. She took up painting instead, and her fiery work, influenced by Mexican folk art, was very popular. She had a turbulent marriage to Mexico's **Diego Rivera**.

Self Portrait with Monkey, 1938. Frida Kahlo once lived with the Russian revolutionary Trotsky, who was assassinated while at her house.

Kandinsky, Wassily

(1866-1944)
Kandinsky was a Russian-born painter who was one of the first artists ever to paint a completely non-representational or **abstract** painting. He said that he returned to his studio one day and was struck by a painting 'of extraordinary beauty' only to find that it was one of his own pictures standing on its side. This helped confirm his mystical belief that colour and line could have their own meaning, without needing to represent something else.

Kauffmann, Angelica

(1741-1807)
Angelica Kauffmann was born in Switzerland but settled in London. She specialized in **portraits** and historical scenes and worked on **murals** for famous architects of the day.

kinetic art

Kinetic art is art that moves – such as a **mobile** or figures that are driven by a mechanism. It comes from the Greek word 'kinesis' which means movement.

Kirchner, Ernst Ludwig

(1880-1938)
Kirchner was a German artist who painted the street life of Berlin in vivid contrasting colours.

Kitaj, R. B.

(1932-)
Ron B. Kitaj is an American painter who has spent most of his life in England. At first he was part of the British **pop art** movement, using images from film and photographs. However, his later work explores his Jewish heritage and the sense of loss caused by the holocaust.

Klee, Paul

(1879-1940)
Paul Klee was a Swiss German best known for his playful attitude to art. He was fascinated by children's painting and tried to translate music into colour. He believed there was another world, more real than this one, which we could get in touch with. In later years he suffered from a condition called scleroderma, and as a result his paintings became dark and bitter.

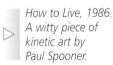

How to Live, 1986. A witty piece of kinetic art by Paul Spooner.

Fulfilment, c. 1905. A gorgeously decorated painting by Klimt.

Klimt, Gustav

(1862-1918)

Gustav Klimt was an Austrian painter and **designer**. His work was very carefully designed and lavishly decorated, often with gold. He loved women and many of his designs celebrated their beauty and mystery.

Kokoschka, Oskar

(1886-1980)

Oskar Kokoschka was born in Austria but also lived in Germany, Britain and Switzerland. He produced **portraits**, **landscapes** and paintings of old myths in a unique style using quick, broad brush strokes. He was forced to leave Germany at the beginning of World War II because of his outspoken opposition to the Nazi Party led by Adolf Hitler.

Koons, Jeff

(1955-)

Jeff Koons is a living American artist who specializes in taking cheap, throwaway objects, such as a silver helium balloon or an ornamental dog, and transforming them into large monuments.

land art

Land art is also sometimes called earth art or earthwork. It is the name given to work which an artist has made from raw materials such as earth, stone and sand. Often land art is made outside so that the work is part of the landscape. **Andy Goldsworthy** is a British artist who works in this form.

landscape

A landscape is a picture of an area of land or countryside.

The Hayfield, 1855-6, by Ford Madox Brown. A fine example of 19th century landscape painting.

Léger, Fernand

(1881-1955)

Fernand Léger was a French painter who became a member of the **cubist** movement. However, instead of the fragments and broken shapes used by **Picasso** and **Braque**, he made his paintings from cylinders and sphere shapes. Someone once called him a 'tubist'! Léger wanted to produce a kind of art that would be a celebration of the modern world, appreciated by anyone, whatever their class or educational background.

Lempicka, Tamara de

(1898-1980)
Tamara de Lempicka was born in Poland but worked as a painter in Paris and New York. Her stylish work, influenced by **Léger**, is still extremely popular – summing up the glamour and gloss of the life of rich people in the 1930s.

Leonardo da Vinci

(1452-1519)
Leonardo da Vinci, the most famous artist of the Italian **Renaissance**, is difficult to sum up because he was so much more than an artist – he was a genius. A **designer**, musician, inventor and scientist, he was fascinated by every detail of the world around him. His notebooks show that he invented flying machines and that he had realized that our planet revolves round the sun long before scientists proved this. To keep his theories secret, Leonardo wrote his notes backwards and with his left hand so that they could only be read in a mirror. His two most famous paintings are 'The Last Supper', which is full of action and character, and the 'Mona Lisa', whose mysterious smile has enchanted viewers for nearly 500 years.

Mona Lisa, c. 1503. This is one of the most famous paintings in the world ever. People find it intriguing because no one knows who this mysterious lady was.

Lichtenstein, Roy

(1923-97)
Roy Lichtenstein was an American pop artist who got his inspiration from children's comics. He enlarged frames of comic strips to a colossal size, reproducing everything, including the dots of the printing process that made up the images. Before developing this style, Lichtenstein painted **abstracts** until one of his young children showed him a comic and challenged him, 'I bet you couldn't paint as good as that!' See also **pop art**.

line

A line is a long thin mark used in drawing to show the shape of an object or a person. A line drawing uses lines only, without shading.

logo

A logo is a special design used by an organization as a kind of badge to distinguish it from other organizations.

Lowry, L. S.

(1887-1976)
Laurence Stephen Lowry was a British painter who spent most of his life painting as a hobby after his normal day's work was finished. During the day he worked as a rent collector and then later as a clerk. At night after work he painted scenes of factories and city streets in the industrial north of England. People often think that Lowry's **cityscapes** with their brooding buildings and armies of stick-like people are charming and humorous, but there is a much darker side to them. They suggest the tiny and miserably thin people are nothing but slaves to the giant industrial machine.

M

Magritte, René

(1898-1967)

Magritte was a Belgian **surrealist** painter who lived what appeared to be a normal, middle-class life in a suburb of Brussels, yet created some of the most disturbing images the art world has ever seen. They have been called 'snapshots of the impossible' – a train coming out of a fireplace, boots with human toes, the sky broken like a pane of glass. In Magritte's pictures, nothing is quite what it seems. He painted them in a very straightforward, impersonal way, which makes their weirdness all the more shocking.

A Bar at the Folies-Bergère, 1881-2. Manet broke the art rules of the time by putting the barmaid right in the centre of the picture. The rest of the scene is reflected in the mirror behind her.

Malevich, Kasimir

(1878-1935)

Malevich was a Russian artist who was one of the first to explore **abstract art**. He used simple, geometric **shapes** and flat colours. Malevich was determined that his paintings should become more pure; this led him to a series entitled 'White on White'. After this, he could go no further and gave up painting.

Man Ray

(1890-1977)

Man Ray was an American artist who, together with **Marcel Duchamp**, set up the New York **Dada** group. He is best known for his photography and photographic spin-offs, and for his **surreal** objects – everyday items with a twist. The best-known of these is an iron with sharp nails sticking out of it.

Manet, Edouard

(1832-83)

Manet was a French painter and one of the founders of **impressionism**. Although his paintings look conventional today, they were revolutionary in his time.

Instead of the carefully controlled, gradual change from light to shade that painters could achieve in their studios, he showed the harsher, more vivid contrasts created by strong sunlight, bleaching out colours and throwing dark, almost black, shadows.

mask

A mask is something you wear over your face. In some cultures masks are used in drama and religious ceremonies so that actors can pretend to be someone else.

A dramatic bird mask made by Kate Hobby aged 12.

Making art, at its simplest, is applying marks, colours and **shapes** onto a surface in order to tell a story or convey an idea or emotion. The original materials used to do this were everyday objects. For instance, cave paintings were drawn with charcoal or burnt wood from the fire and coloured with earths and natural dyes. Most of the paints we now use are manufactured to a very high standard, yet they are still made from the same natural ingredients. Here are some of the materials and equipment that an artist uses today.

materials used for drawing

Pencils are graded between HH for very hard and 6B for soft.
Pen and ink. A natural ink, such as Indian ink, applied with a nib is best for drawing.
Charcoal is made from burnt twigs.
Chalk is a very soft stone.
Pastels are sticks of colour mixed with a weak glue.

A collection of chalks and pastels laid out ready for use.

materials used for painting

Paint is made up of raw pigment or colour mixed with another substance called a medium. The colour comes from ground-up rocks or semi-precious stones or dyes from plants and insects. The medium acts as a kind of glue to bind the powdery pigment together. It also sticks the colour to the surface of the painting.

Watercolour comes in tubes or blocks. It is mixed and thinned with water and makes transparent washes of colour.

Gouache is a watercolour paint that has been mixed with white to make it opaque. It makes a flat, even colour.

Acrylic paint is sold in tubes. It is a relatively new type of paint which behaves like oil paint but can be mixed with water.

Tempera is pigment mixed with egg. It forms transparent layers of strong colour.

Encaustic paint is mixed with hot wax.

Pastel (also a material for drawing) is a stick of colour mixed with a weak glue.

Oil pastel is a new material made by adding an oily material to the glue medium.

Oil paint is supplied in tubes and is pure colour mixed with oil. It can be thinned with spirit solvents such as turpentine or white spirit.

tools and equipment

There are many ways of applying colours and shapes to make a painting. Artists have traditionally used brushes or palette knives. However, today's mixed-media work can often require the use of other tools. Here are some of the most widely used.

brushes

These come in a variety of shapes and sizes. They can be made from animal hair or artificial fibres. Soft brushes are made from sable, squirrel, pony, ox or camel and are used for delicate work done with thin paint. Hard or stiff brushes are used for covering large areas with thicker paint. They are made with bristle from a pig, goat or badger. Larger areas can be painted with the same kind of brushes used for painting houses. Here is a range of the most useful brushes: round, mop, flat, short flat or bright, filbert, fan handle and ferrule hair.

palette knife

These soft, bendy blades are used for mixing paint. They can also be used instead of a brush to lay paint onto a surface very thickly.

palette

Any hard, waterproof surface can be used for laying out paint in various colours and mixing them to make different **shades** and **tints**. Because watercolour paints are so runny, the palette should have shallow pans to stop them running off the surface.

dipper

These are small pots that clip onto the edge of a palette. They can hold water, oil or paint thinner.

mahlstick

This long stick is used to steady the artist's hand when the paint is wet.

easel

The easel is designed to hold the painting still, in one position, while it is being worked on. It is not an essential piece of equipment. Many artists use a board propped on a table.

lay figure

This is a jointed wooden figure that can be moved into any pose to help the artist to draw without a model. It can be of a person, a body part such as a hand, or an animal such as a horse.

surfaces used in painting

A painting has to be made on some kind of surface, which is sometimes called a support. It can be anything from traditional canvas stretched over a wooden frame, to a wall or a piece of paper. The surfaces of the support can also be treated with another substance so that it takes the paint better. Here are some of the surfaces that can be used: wood (including plywood, blockboard, chipboard, hardboard and M.D.F.); cloth (including linen, cotton, hessian and canvas; paper and card (some papers are specially made for watercolour painting); walls, usually treated with plaster or plasterboard; any other flat surface, such as stone, metal, glass, plastic or even ordinary household furniture.

Matisse, Henri

(1869-1954)

Matisse was a French painter who drew inspiration from the bright colours of the Mediterranean. Although he lived through two world wars nothing ugly entered his painted world. He wanted viewers to sink into his paintings like 'a good armchair'. In his later years he made spectacular pictures from pieces of coloured paper. He said 'instead of drawing the outline and putting in the colour' now he was able to 'draw in the colour'.

Michelangelo

(1475-1564)

Michelangelo was an Italian sculptor and painter of the **Renaissance** who lived at the same time as **Leonardo da Vinci**. He was fascinated by the human body. By studying anatomy (dissecting bodies himself) he learned how to draw people from every angle, moving or still. Not only were his figures accurate, they also seemed full of life. His first love was sculpture, and he **carved** some of the most life-like marble statues ever produced. Among them is his **nude** figure of David. His most famous work was the painted ceiling of the Sistine Chapel in the Vatican. He completed this large and complicated job in just four years, lying on his back on scaffolding.

The Creation of Adam, 1510. The brilliant centre-piece of Michelangelo's Sistine Chapel ceiling.

Millais, John Everett

(1829-96)

The British painter Millais was one of the founders of the **Pre-Raphaelite Brotherhood**. He was a very gifted child and, at the age of 11, was the youngest person ever to be given a place at the Royal Academy schools. Later in life he moved away from the precise, detailed style of the Pre-Raphaelites and began to paint popular, sentimental pictures which earned him a great deal of money.

Millet, Jean François

(1814-75)

Millet was a French painter, and was unusual for his time because he painted peasants at work, rather than comfortable rich people. He wanted to show that their ordinary, everyday lives were as important as anyone else's.

miniature

Miniature means very small. In the art world, a miniature is a tiny painting, usually a **portrait** that is small enough to be held in the hand or worn as a piece of jewellery.

minimalism

Minimal means 'hardly anything'. Minimal art is a kind of **abstract art** in which everything is made as simple as possible. Artists are deliberately trying not to express any emotions but to concentrate on the colours and **shapes**.

Miró, Joan

(1893-1983)

Miró was a Spanish painter who divided his time mostly between Paris and Barcelona. He is famous for his semi-**abstract** pictures, full of crescent **shapes**, squiggles and **forms** that could be people, animals or amoebas. The **surrealists** counted him as one of their members, though Miró did not wish to join any group. Miró's pictures inspired many of the displays at the opening ceremony of the Barcelona Olympics in 1992. See also **surrealism**.

mixed media

A work of art is described as having been made in mixed media if an artist uses a combination of materials (media) to make it.

mobile

A mobile is a sculpture that moves. It is usually made of flat **shapes** or objects, which are suspended so that they can swing freely in the air.

model

In the art world a model is a person who gets paid for posing (usually **nude**) to be drawn or painted in a studio.

Modigliani, Amedeo

(1884-1920)

Modigliani was an Italian sculptor and painter who worked mostly in Paris. He lived life at an exhausting pace, endangering his health with drink and drugs. He was impressed by African masks which influenced his long, sculpted heads and his paintings of **nudes** – two subjects he returned to again and again. He died of tuberculosis in his mid-30s.

Mondrian, Piet

(1872-1944)

Mondrian was a Dutch painter famous for his simple, **abstract** paintings made entirely of rectangles and squares of white and primary colours. He began painting from nature, wanting to discover an art that was purely spiritual. In a famous series of paintings of an apple tree, Mondrian introduced a grid of lines. With each picture, the grid began to take over until the tree disappeared altogether.

Monet, Claude

(1840-1926)

Monet was a French painter and the founder of the **impressionists**. He was very interested in the effect of light on objects and **landscapes** and wanted to capture it in his work. To do this he painted in the open air and – because light changes so quickly – he worked rapidly and developed a style of painting using fast dabs or strokes of colour. At the time people thought his pictures looked slapdash or unfinished. Now, people appreciate these lovely impressions of light and colour.

A mobile made from found objects by Kate Hobby aged 12.

White Water Lilies, 1889. Monet loved to paint the water garden at his house in Giverny, France.

N

monochrome

A monochrome painting is made using various **shades** of one colour only.

Moore, Henry

(1898-1986)
Henry Moore was the son of a Yorkshire miner who became a famous British sculptor. He loved natural objects like pebbles, bones, shells and driftwood and he wanted his **sculpture** to have the same feel. When he **carved** wood or stone, he allowed the material to influence how the piece turned out. So he would be more likely to shape a stone that looked like a woman than to carve a woman out of stone.

▷ *Family Group 1948-9 by Henry Moore.*

△ *Mosaic by Oliver Matthews, Mungo Pay, Nathaniel Sherbourne and Jos Spafford-Baker, all aged 11.*

mosaic

A mosaic is a picture or **design** made up of small pieces of coloured tile set in mortar.

Munch, Edvard

(1863-1944)
Munch was a Norwegian painter. He had a difficult childhood which left him mentally unstable. His powerful, emotional work is full of themes such as jealousy, illness, death and fear.

mural

A mural is a picture painted on a wall.

▷ *The Scream, 1893. Everything in Munch's famous painting works together to create a feeling of painful emotion.*

naive art

Naive art is the term used for work made by artists who are untrained and who paint naturally in a child-like way.

narrative art

Narrative art describes paintings or **sculptures** that tell a story.

Nicholson, Ben

(1894-1982)
Ben Nicholson was a British painter who specialized in painted **abstract reliefs**. He was one of the earliest and foremost painters of abstracts in Britain. He was married to the sculptor **Barbara Hepworth** and they were at the centre of the group of artists living in St Ives, Cornwall.

Bather and Sand Castle, 1945. Sidney Nolan.

Nolan, Sidney

(1917-92)
Sidney Nolan is probably Australia's most famous artist. He has a very personal style of painting – his brightly coloured pictures capture the brilliant blue sky and fierce heat of the sun-baked land. Nolan is best known for his paintings featuring the notorious Australian gangster Ned Kelly wearing his legendary metal helmet.

Nolde, Emil

(1867-1956)
Emil Nolde was a German painter who worked on scenes from the Bible which were full of intense emotions and distorted figures in violent colours. His **landscapes** also displayed powerful emotions but were calmer. In 1941 the Nazi Party (led by Adolf Hitler) ordered him to stop painting, but Nolde carried on producing small watercolours in secret until the war was over.

nude

A painting, photograph or sculpture of a person with no clothes on.

O'Keeffe, Georgia

(1887-1986)
Georgia O'Keeffe was an American painter best known for her magnified, **abstract** paintings of flowers and plant **forms**. Sometimes they are so big that they could almost be **landscapes**.

old master

When an artist or craftsman finished his training in medieval times, he became 'Master' of a guild (an organization of skilled people). An old master is the name that we give to a recognized artist from the past.

Oldenburg, Claes

(1929-)
Oldenburg was born in Sweden but has lived most of his life in America. Part of the **pop art** movement, he is best known for his gigantic sculptures of junk food and for his 'soft sculptures'. In real life the things that he sculpted would be hard objects, such as a light switch, but Oldenburg would make one a hundred times the size, out of a soft material such as vinyl.

op art

The term 'op art' is short for 'optical art'. It is usually **abstract** work, made up of some combination of **lines** or **shapes**, which create an unusual or interesting visual effect. **Bridget Riley** is one of the most famous op artists.

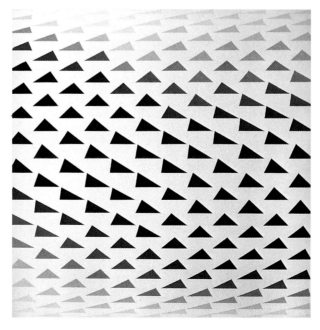

Turn, 1964. Bridget Riley

Chinese and Japanese art

The Imperial Dynasties of China

Shang	1480 - 1050 BC
Zhou	1122 - 256 BC
(Warring States	481 - 221 BC)
Qin (Ch'in)	221 - 206 BC
Han	202 - AD 220
Jin (Tsin)	AD 265 - 316
Sui	AD 589 - 618
Tang	AD 618 - 907
Song (Sung)	AD 960 - 1127
(in south only	AD 1127 - 1279)
Yuan (Mongol)	AD 1271 - 1368
Ming	AD 1368 - 1644
Qung (Manchu)	AD 1644 - 1911

early Chinese arts

China's earliest dynasties – the Shang and Zhou – grew up around the Yellow River. They developed the distinctive Chinese writing style, and produced works of art in bronze, pottery, jade and silk. The Qin and Han dynasties are especially known for their tomb sculptures. When powerful people were buried, ceramic figures of servants and soldiers were left with the body to help them in the afterlife. Other artistic discoveries included lacquer work, silk weaving and glazing for pottery. Around AD 500 Hsieh Ho developed the 'six principles of painting' which have dominated Chinese work ever since.

▷ Chinese pottery figure of a woman from the Tang period.

△ Enamelled porcelain vase from the Qung dynasty

the dynasties

The Tang dynasty was a golden age for Chinese art. Porcelain was discovered and pottery could be glazed in two and three colours. (See also **decorative arts.**) Long hand-scrolls and hanging scrolls featured the art of painting and handwriting, or calligraphy. Buddhist-inspired 'mountain and water' **landscape** painting developed strongly in the Song dynasty, with tiny people in vast expanses of country showing just how insignificant people are in relation to nature. The Mongol dynasty of Yuan developed carving in red lacquer. They also inspired much Buddhist sculpture.

The court art of the Ming dynasty is legendary for its use of rich colours and decoration in painting. They also developed the mass production of decorated ceramic work, lacquer work, mother-of-pearl inlay and cloisonné enamelling, all of which became prized throughout the world.

△ Painting of a lotus flower on silk by Yun Shou-ping, 1633-90, Qung dynasty.

Japan

The earliest works of art found in Japan were pots with **patterns** of raised lines, tomb figures made of clay and engraved bronze bells. The introduction of the Buddhist religion meant that Japan adopted some things from Chinese culture after AD 500, but used them in a uniquely Japanese style. The art of Japanese scroll painting developed, showing historical tales and legends. Zen Buddhism emphasized nature, developing the arts of landscape gardening, **architecture** and pottery for the tea ceremony.

▽ Boats Caught in a Great Wave off Kanazawa, 1831. Hokusai is the master of the Japanese woodcut.

▽ A Japanese kimono.

Japanese **printmaking** developed in the Edo period when artists such as **Hokusai** and Utamaro became very popular. Their work was particularly admired by the Western painters who came after the **impressionists**.

△ Late 18th century Japanese lacquered wood box with coral and shell decoration.

P

painterly

Artists' work is described as painterly if they are interested not only in the image that they are producing but also in the texture and surface of the paint.

Palmer, Samuel

(1805-81)
Samuel Palmer was a British **landscape** painter and etcher. He is best known for the strange, almost magical paintings and **prints** he made. He claimed he had visions and strange experiences from childhood – something he shared with **William Blake**, whom he met at the age of 17.

patron

A patron is a person who asks an artist to make a special piece of work and pays for it.

pattern

A pattern is a **design** or decoration where the shapes are repeated.

A bird pattern by Jack Brougham aged 13.

performance art

This is a form of art using people rather than paint to demonstrate an idea. Works are 'performed', usually in front of an audience. The Dadaists and surrealists in the early 20th century were the first to use performance to shock people and to draw attention to their work. It was not until the 1960s and 70s that performance art came to be recognized as an art form in its own right. See also **Dada**, **surrealism**.

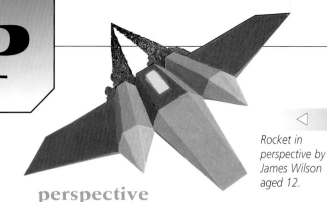

Rocket in perspective by James Wilson aged 12.

perspective

Perspective is a method of drawing that artists use to give an impression of distance. They do this by making objects smaller the further away they are, and by making parallel lines (such as railway tracks) appear to get closer together in the distance.

photomontage

Photomontage uses parts of photographs placed together to make up a new image.

Brooklyn Bridge, 1982. Artist David Hockney's photomontage. You can see his feet at the bottom of the picture.

Picasso, Pablo

(1881-1973)
Pablo Picasso is probably the most famous artist of the 20th century. Born in Spain, he spent a great deal of his working life in France. Along with his friend **Georges Braque**, Picasso invented **cubism**, a different way of looking at objects that caused a revolution in art. His work was full of enormous energy and passion. His moving and disturbing 1937 painting 'Guernica', which was a protest at the bombing by Fascists of the Basque capital during the Spanish Civil War, is one of the most memorable images of the 20th century.

Guernica, 1937. Picasso's enormous painting is an angry statement against the horrors of war.

Picasso is best known as a painter but his sculpture was also extremely imaginative and sometimes witty. He often used things he had found – such as a bicycle saddle, or a toy car – and with just a twist or a small addition turned them into works of art. He continued to work well into old age and when he had become immensely rich and successful. He left behind him a staggering 20,000 works of art!

Piero della Francesca

(1410/20-1492)
The Italian painter Piero della Francesca was better known during his lifetime as a mathematician than as a painter. However, his religious paintings combine a wonderfully clear **design** with a strong sense of colour and light. His best-known work is a series of **frescoes** on the legend of the true cross. In later years he became a court **portrait** painter, until his failing eyesight caused him to give up painting and concentrate on mathematics.

Pissarro, Camille

(1830-1903)
Pissarro was a French painter, born in the West Indies. His paintings were made using rapid strokes in vibrant colours and he helped to develop the ideas behind **impressionism**. He was a kind of father figure to the other impressionist painters and was a very good teacher. Among others, he taught **Cézanne** and **Gauguin**. Later in his career he also began to use some of the techniques of **pointillism**. In old age his eyesight grew worse and he was restricted to painting **cityscapes** from the window of his room in Paris. He died blind.

Detail of Seurat's pointillist painting, Bathers at Asnières.

pointillism

This is a technique of building up a painting by using many small dots of pure colour. From a distance the dots fuse together to make a misty overall effect. Often primary colours, such as blue and yellow, are placed next to each other so that the viewer's eye appears to 'mix' them into green. The 19th century French artist **Seurat** was the first painter to use this technique.

Pollock, Jackson

(1912-56)

Pollock was an American painter who was best known for his controversial 'drip and splash' style. *Time* magazine called him 'Jack the Dripper'. He would lay his canvas on the floor and pour paint directly onto the surface from a can. Rather than use brushes he would use sticks, trowels and knives to drip and spread the paint. He also used other materials such as sand and broken glass to provide extra texture. Pollock was the first and most important member of the school of **abstract expressionism**. He was trying to express his true feelings directly through the paint. The result was a series of powerful, highly energetic, **abstract** paintings. For most of his life he struggled with a tendency to drink too much and an unhappy personal life. He died in a car crash at the age of 44.

Portrait of Catherine Duchess of Suffolk, 1532-43 by Hans Holbein.

pop art

Pop art was a popular art movement that began in the 1950s and lasted until the early 1970s – most of its followers were in the USA and Britain. Artists began to look at the everyday products that surrounded them such as Coke bottles, soup cans and popular magazines. Even though these things were often thought of as cheap and tasteless, pop artists believed that since they were an important part of our world they should be a subject for art. Some of the best-known pop artists are **Peter Blake**, **Roy Lichtenstein**, **Claes Oldenburg** and **Andy Warhol**.

portrait

A portrait is a picture of a person.

Poussin, Nicolas

(1594-1665)

Poussin was a French painter in the classical tradition. He was fascinated by stories of ancient Greece and Rome and painted representations of them in a careful, controlled manner. He was so concerned to get everything right that he would sometimes make wax models of the figures for his pictures, and place them on something like a theatrical stage to check the **composition** and light.

Whaam!, 1963. Roy Lichtenstein's popular pop art painting is based on a 1950s war comic.

Pre-Raphaelite Brotherhood

The Pre-Raphaelite Brotherhood was a group of young British painters who formed this secret society in 1848. They rebelled against what they thought of as the dull, traditional standards of the art world which saw **Raphael** as the standard of everything that was good. Among the best-known Pre-Raphaelites were **Holman Hunt** and **Millais**. They wanted a return to sincerity and simplicity. They painted moral stories and **religious** pictures, trying to get every natural detail accurate. They claimed to hate sentimental pictures, but somehow ended up painting them.

Ophelia, 1851. John Everett Millais painted the dying heroine of Shakespeare's play Hamlet.

print

A print is made when an artist cuts an image into something like a metal plate, or a piece of wood or lino. The design is covered in printing ink and pressed onto paper or cloth, often using a roller or a printing press.

quattrocento

Quattrocento is the Italian word for the number 400. It is used in connection with Italian art of the 1400s when the **Renaissance** was at its height.

Madonna and Child with the Infant Baptist, 1509. The Virgin Mary looks calmly on as the two children play in Raphael's picture.

Raphael

(1483-1520)
For many years after his death the Italian painter Raphael was considered to be the greatest painter who ever lived. He set the standard for generations of art students, and thousands of them have copied his work. Raphael himself lived and worked at the same time as **Leonardo da Vinci** and **Michelangelo** but stands out from them because of the calm, serenity and simplicity of his pictures. This may have sprung from his own personality which was amiable and easy-going. The people he painted looked beautiful, healthy and at ease – they showed a kind of ideal lifestyle. He was immensely popular in his own lifetime and when he died at the tragically young age of 37, it was reported that even the Pope cried.

Rauschenberg, Robert

(1925-)
Robert Rauschenberg lives in New York and finds inspiration for his 'combine' paintings on the city streets. He likes to pick up odd things from junk shops and puts them together into works of art. He is particularly fond of coming across things by accident. For example, when he found some unlabelled tins of paint one day, he decided to use them no matter what colour was inside. His best-known work is 'Monogram', featuring a paint-spattered stuffed goat with a car tyre round its middle.

relief

A relief is a form of **sculpture** which is carved from one side of a flat panel. It is usually mounted on a wall.

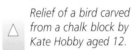

religious art

Religious art is sometimes made to help people to worship, or it can simply be a way of showing a story with a religious theme. Art has always been closely linked to mythology and religion. The very earliest kinds of art may have been made to play a part in religious ritual. Many scholars think prehistoric cave paintings of animals were made in the hope that they might give the cave dwellers magic power over the creatures they hunted.

In ancient civilizations all over the world, priests or shamans commissioned works of art or produced art themselves as part of their rituals. For example, the wonderfully decorated tombs of the Egyptian kings were inspired by religious belief. For many hundreds of years, most of the art in Europe was Christian religious art. This did not mean that artists were necessarily more religious than other people, but that the Christian story was considered to be the most important subject for art at the time. Also, the Church was able to afford large and expensive pieces.

In the 1500s there was a dramatic change when – following the Protestant Reformation – many Protestant thinkers taught that religious images should not be made. They thought people would worship the art, rather than the God who inspired it. From this point on many artists began to paint non-religious subjects. Today, artists still make religious art, but it is usually to express their personal beliefs.

Relief of a bird carved from a chalk block by Kate Hobby aged 12.

Rembrandt van Rijn

(1606-69)

The Dutch painter Rembrandt van Rijn is considered alongside such artists as **Raphael**, **Michelangelo** and **Picasso** to be one of the greatest artists who ever lived. What makes his sombre, often dark, pictures stand out is his understanding of people. He spent the early part of his life as a **portrait** painter (his honest series of self-portraits are a revealing story in themselves) and his work gives a sense of knowing the real character of the sitter.

Although he was very successful, Rembrandt understood hardship and tragedy. Almost all his children died as infants and only one outlived him. When his wife Saskia died, Rembrandt was unable to marry Hendrickje, the woman he fell in love with afterwards, because of a clause in Saskia's will. Finally he was declared bankrupt.

Self portrait c. 1665. Rembrandt painted many portraits of himself. This one shows him as an old man.

In spite of these difficulties, he had a profound religious faith and a genuine love of the Bible. In his later years he stopped painting portraits and spent a large part of his time exploring the stories of the Bible in **drawings**, paintings and etchings (he was a master etcher). He seemed to be able to get under the skin of the characters in these stories and make them come alive. The darkness of the paintings gave the rare bright colours an extra glow.

Renaissance

Renaissance is an Italian word that means 'rebirth'. Italian artists and thinkers of the 14th century believed that they were reviving the values of the classical world of the ancient Greeks and Romans. They despised the art and **architecture** that had developed in the period they called 'the middle age' (and which we still call the Middle Ages or medieval times).

Three very creative people were at the heart of this revival – the architect Brunelleschi, the painter Masaccio and the sculptor **Donatello** – all of whom knew each other and were based in Florence.

Renaissance artists were fascinated by individual human beings, rather than the larger issues such as religion. This fascination led to the study of anatomy and other scientific explorations. Over the years, Renaissance thinking spread from Florence to other cities such as Venice and Rome. At its high point between 1500 and the 1520s – known as the High Renaissance – artistic giants like **Leonardo**, **Michelangelo** and **Raphael** were all working in Rome at the same time.

Renoir, Pierre-Auguste

(1841-1919)
Renoir was a French painter and a leading light in the school of **impressionism**. He was a close friend of **Monet**. Renoir is one of the most popular of the impressionists

because of his light-hearted, pretty scenes and portraits – particularly his soft, rounded **nudes**, painted with feathery brush strokes. Renoir said, 'Why shouldn't art be pretty? There are enough unpleasant things in the world.'

Riley, Bridget

(1931-)
Bridget Riley is the leading British artist making **op art**. She is very skilled at using optical effects through **line** and colour – able to produce a visual buzz and trick the eye with huge paintings.

Rivera, Diego

(1886-1957)
Diego Rivera was a Mexican artist who specialized in gigantic wall paintings. He was a socialist and wanted his work to express his political beliefs. His huge paintings draw on Mexican folk traditions, and celebrate the history and people of Mexico. They show workers as heroes, and the bosses as enemies. He had a turbulent life with the painter **Frida Kahlo**, whom he married twice.

Ball at the Moulin de la Galette, 1876. Renoir painted many of his friends at the famous Parisian dance hall.

Rodin, Auguste

(1840-1917)

Rodin was a French **sculptor** who worked around the same time as the **impressionists**. 'The Kiss' and 'The Thinker' are his most famous pieces. He liked to leave part of the marble rough and unfinished as a contrast with the smooth suppleness of his figures.

Rodin's famous sculpture, The Thinker, c. 1880.

Rothko, Mark

(1903-70)

Mark Rothko was a Russian-born painter who lived and worked in America. His huge paintings are made up of soft, blurred-edged rectangles of intense, shifting colours that seem to float on the canvas like clouds. In later life he made a series of paintings for the walls and ceiling of a non-denominational chapel in Texas. Although their effect can be calming, Rothko put a great deal of his own emotions and torment into his paintings. In the end, he committed suicide in his studio.

Rousseau, Henri

(1844-1910)

The French painter Henri Rousseau was known as the 'customs officer' because he worked for the customs office and did not start painting until he was 40. He is probably the most famous of all **naive** artists – his pictures have a dream-like, childish atmosphere. He is best known for his jungle paintings, which he claimed came from trips he made to Mexico, but he probably made them up from visits to the botanical gardens and the zoo.

Rubens, Peter Paul

(1577-1640)

Peter Paul Rubens was a Flemish painter, famous for his chubby, pink, **nude** women (it was not fashionable to be slim in the 17th century). He was an extremely skilful and successful artist, a master of **portraits**, **narrative** paintings and **landscape**. Rubens was so much in demand for work that he ran a studio that was almost like an art factory – with many assistants working under his direction.

Ruisdael, Jacob van

(1628/9-82)

Not a great deal is known about this Dutch **landscape** painter except that he painted some of the finest scenes produced in the whole of the 17th century. The scenes are full of mood and atmosphere – often suggested by the play of light on the scene and the hint of movement in the clouds.

Ruskin, John

(1819-1900)

John Ruskin was a British **critic**, writer and watercolourist. He believed art was important for working people, and hated the way the industrial revolution was killing off old crafts. His personal life was unhappy and he suffered from mental illness in later life.

Tropical Storm with a Tiger (Surprised!), 1891. Rousseau's painting of a jungle.

Saint Phalle, Niki de

(1930-)
Niki de Saint Phalle, the French sculptor, is responsible for one work which is more famous than anything else she has done. It is an enormous reclining woman which she created in Stockholm with the help of **Jean Tinguely**. Painted in gaudy colours on the outside, it is so big that visitors can walk around inside. There is a milkbar inside, and a cinema showing Greta Garbo films.

Salon

For hundreds of years France's only public art exhibition was held in the Salon d'Apollon in the Louvre. By the 19th century it had become very conservative, so that new, creative artists could not get their work accepted. This gave rise to alternatives, such as the Salon des Refusés (for those refused entry), and the Salon des Indépendants (for 'independents'). See also **galleries and museums**.

Schwitters, Kurt

(1887-1948)
Kurt Schwitters was a German artist and poet who was a leading member of the **Dada** movement. His speciality was making art out of non-art. He began by using rubbish from the streets – bus tickets, envelopes, bits of string – and making them into **collages**, which reflected the throwaway life of the city. Later he made large-scale constructions including one huge piece of work that took up two floors of his house in Hanover.

S sculpture

A sculpture is a piece of art made in three dimensions rather than two. In other words, you can walk round it. Traditionally, sculpture is either carved out of a material such as stone or wood, or cast in bronze or some similar metal. Some of the most famous sculptors of the past include **Donatello**, **Michelangelo**, **Rodin** and **Henry Moore**.

Head sculpted from a breeze block by Jack Brougham aged 13.

When sculptures are of people, they are usually called statues. Most cities have statues of famous people who have a connection to the area. There are also famous statues, such as 'the discus thrower' from ancient Greece, which are so old that we have no way of knowing who made them. In the 20th century sculptors have tried to find other ways of working – especially when creating a likeness to a person is not the main point. They have tried different materials such as plastic and glass, large sheets of metal welded together or even things that other people have thrown away.

Seascape by Thea Wright aged 8.

seascape

A seascape is a painting of the sea or a view of the shoreline.

Seurat, Georges

(1859-91)
Seurat was a French painter and the inventor of what has become known as **pointillism**. Fascinated by the work of the **impressionists**, he set out to find a scientific way of getting the same sort of effect. He did this by putting small dabs of pure colour close to each other like a **mosaic**. In order that viewers could make out what he was painting, he made all the **shapes** in his pictures very simple. This gives his work a sense of stillness, while the dots of paint give it a hazy quality.

△ *Bathers at Asnières, 1883 by the pointillist Seurat.*

shade

A shade is a darker version of a **colour**, made by mixing it with black.

shape

Shape is similar in meaning to **form**. It is used to describe the measurements or dimensions of an object. For example, the shape of a ball is round.

Sickert, Walter

(1860-1942)
Sickert was a British painter who was influenced by the **impressionists** and at one time worked with **Degas**. He once said art should 'avoid the drawing room and stick to the kitchen', meaning that it should be about working people and normal life. Sickert often chose urban scenes in dark sombre colours, beautifully painted in broad, loose brush strokes. He has been a strong influence on British painting, because of his love of domestic scenes and because his colours reflect the British climate.

sketch

A sketch is a rough, usually quick **drawing**. Artists often use sketches as notes for a bigger, more finished piece of work.

◁ *Sketch by Laura Thompson-Lynch aged 11.*

Smith, David

(1906-65)
David Smith was an American sculptor, famous for his massive work using boxes and cylinders of polished steel, often precariously balanced on one another. As a young man he had been employed in a car factory where he learned steel-working skills.

space

Space is the empty gap between one thing and another. You get a space between two lines on a page or two **shapes** in a painting. Artists take as much care about leaving spaces as they do about painting shapes. Sculptors are also careful about the way their **sculptures** stand in an empty space.

Spencer, Stanley

(1891-1959)
Stanley Spencer was an imaginative and eccentric British painter. He is best known for his pictures of biblical stories set in the streets and houses of his own village of Cookham, in Berkshire, England.

still life

A still life is a painting of a group of objects that are not alive and cannot move. A typical still life might be a bowl of fruit or other food on a table, but it could equally be a dead animal or a pile of books.

Still life with water melon by Rhiannon Davies aged 12.

Stubbs, George

(1724-1806)
George Stubbs was a British painter who specialized in horses. He studied animal anatomy and published a famous volume of beautiful engravings. He was in great demand to paint the favourite animals of rich landowners.

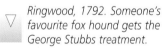

Ringwood, 1792. Someone's favourite fox hound gets the George Stubbs treatment.

studio

A studio is an artist's workshop. Studios often have windows facing north, because this provides a constant light, less affected by the position of the sun in the sky.

study

A study is a **drawing** or painting made as a preparation for a larger work.

style

Style in art is the particular way an artist or a group of artists do their work. For example, painters who follow the style of **expressionism** use bold brush strokes to show how they feel about what they are painting.

surrealism

Surrealism was an art movement popular in the 1920s and 1930s. Its followers were fascinated by people's unconscious minds and how they work. The art they produced was full of bizarre objects and images, and things that wouldn't normally fit together – such as a telephone made from a lobster. Some of the most famous surrealists were **Salvador Dali**, **René Magritte** and **Giorgio de Chirico**.

Sutherland, Graham

(1903-80)
Graham Sutherland was a British painter who – though he painted **landscapes** and was an official **war artist** – is most remembered for his **portraits** and his **religious art**. His portraits were not always popular – Lady Spencer Churchill destroyed Sutherland's portrait of Sir Winston Churchill because she disliked it so much. His most acclaimed work is the enormous tapestry 'Christ in Glory' in Coventry Cathedral.

Techniques

A technique is simply a way of doing something. Over the centuries artists have used the tools and **materials** available in their own time to invent new ways of working with **form**, **line**, **shape**, texture and **colour** to produce a particular effect. Today young artists learn about popular existing ways of doing things so that they can continue to invent new techniques based on the knowledge of other artists who went before them.

painting

Painting is the action of putting colours onto a surface so that they form shapes or a picture. The colours themselves come from natural materials such as ground-up semi-precious stones, rocks and earths, or dyes extracted from plants and insects. Today, paints are made using chemical processes but the materials are basically the same.

△ *Oil pastel, child artist (unknown).*

Whatever surface the artist chooses (paper, canvas, silk, board, etc.) has to be prepared before it can be painted. It can be primed with a ground of paint, or a thicker surface called gesso can be built up by painting on layers of a chalky substance and rubbing each one down until it is smooth. To begin a painting, the artist usually makes a **drawing** or **sketch** using pencil, charcoal or a thin paint. This may be followed by a layer of 'underpainting' or 'lay-in'. At this stage, the whole might be painted in shades of one colour, so that the artist can work out which are the lighter and deeper **tones**.

Next the colour is put on with a brush or palette knife. A layer of thick colour mixed with white is called body colour. If the paint is very thick it is called impasto. To scumble is to drag paint thinly over the surface leaving gaps. A thin, transparent covering of paint is called a wash or frottie. This can be put on with a brush, or by rubbing with a rag or even with the fingers. Other effects can be achieved by dabbing paint on with a textured object like a sponge, or blending colours into each other where they meet. Artists can also stipple paint in dots, tease out the paint when it is just drying and spray or spatter paint onto the surface. Shadows can be made by hatching and cross hatching parallel lines of paint across each other.

△ *Acrylic painting, child artist (unknown).*

Special effects can be added using a texture such as sand, or by sticking materials or objects to the surface – called **collage**. Paint can also be taken away by scraping back to the previous colour with a knife, pulling off the surface with a dry sponge or rag, or sgraffito, scratching or scoring into wet paint with a hard object.

Other shapes can be added to a picture using a cut-out card as a guard or stencil. The hard-edge style of painting in flat colours and geometric shapes is achieved by masking off areas of the painting with tape.

A painting is often finished by glazing, varnishing or spraying with fixative. This is a transparent layer that protects the paint and adds richness to the colour.

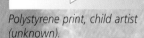

Polystyrene print, child artist (unknown).

printmaking

Processes for making prints have developed because they allow artists to make copies of their work at low cost. The simplest form of print, called relief engraving, is where the design is cut into a material such as a half-potato, a strip of lino or a block of wood. The raised surface is coated with colour ready for printing. In more complicated techniques such as intaglio, etching, aquatint and mezzotint the designs are cut into a metal plate. These techniques can produce much more detailed images than relief engraving. The plate is inked and wiped so that the colour only remains in the cuts. Screen printing reproduces a **pattern** or **design** directly from one flat surface to another, often using wax and ink.

△ *Painting on silk by Lucy Parker aged 12.*

sculpture and modelling

Sculpture involves making anything in three dimensions. Painting and drawing are usually flat (two-dimensional), whereas you can walk all the way round a three-dimensional object such as a statue. The three basic methods of making a sculpture are carving, modelling and construction.

Carving involves cutting away material from a block until the **shape** is revealed. A picture carved into a flat panel is called a bas-relief. Modelling is when an artist builds up the shape from soft materials such as clay, wax or papier mâché. The shape can be supported by a frame of chickenwire, wood or any other sturdy material. Copies of a clay or wax model can then be made by casting them in metal, (see **sculpture**). Three-dimensional objects can also be constructed by joining together separate parts or found objects with glue or welding.

▷ *Papier mâché model by Melissa Orrom Swan.*

T

Tatlin, Vladimir

(1885-1953)

Vladimir Tatlin was a Russian painter and construction maker who was part of the Constructivist movement in the early years of the Russian Revolution. He believed art should be made from materials that workers used – such as glass, steel and timber. His most famous construction was 'Monument to the Third International'. This was a model of an enormous tower in the shape of a leaning spiral, which was to be 30 metres taller than the Eiffel Tower. Unfortunately there were doubts about whether it would stand up safely and it was never built.

textile

A textile is any woven cloth or fabric.

△ Textile lizard on a batik background, by Clare Battle aged 11.

Tiepolo, Giovanni Battista

(1696-1770)

Tiepolo was the last of the great Italian **fresco** painters. His paintings decorated the walls and ceilings of palaces and the houses of the rich and famous. His work was light and airy, full of joy and frivolity.

Tinguely, Jean

(1925-91)

Jean Tinguely was a Swiss sculptor who made extraordinary machines. He wanted to poke fun at the idea of industry and technology and so constructed elaborate, useless pieces of moving machinery, some of which were designed to destroy themselves. One of his best-known pieces is a joint venture with **Niki de Saint Phalle** – a series of strange water-spouting machines in a pool outside the Pompidou Centre in Paris.

tint

A tint is a lighter or paler version of a colour, made by mixing it with white – so pink is a tint of red.

Tintoretto

(1518-94)

Tintoretto was an Italian painter who worked in Venice. His real name was Jacopo Robusti – Tintoretto was a nickname taken from his father's profession as a dyer of cloth (a 'tintore'). Tintoretto was unusual for his time in that he painted with quick, almost rough, brush strokes and made the viewer look at the scenes he painted from an unusual point of view. His religious and mythological scenes have a powerful sense of drama and excitement.

Titian

(c.1485-1576)

The Italian painter Titian was recognized as a genius in his own lifetime. He lived and worked in Venice, where he painted many of the most famous people of his time. One story says that he was so well respected that when he dropped a brush, King Charles V bent down and picked it up for him (Kings in those days never stooped to pick up anything!). He is admired most for his use of colour. Today, deep red-orange hair is called 'titian' after him.

tonal painting

A painting in tones of brown, black and white with only a rare splash of colour.

tone

Tone is a technical term to do with **colour**. If you mix grey (a mixture of black and white) with any other colour it alters its tone. The new tone will depend on how dark or light the grey was (in other words, how much black or white there was in the grey). More generally, people talk about the tone of a colour to mean how bright it is. So someone might say, 'You need a darker tone of blue to make the yellow stand out'.

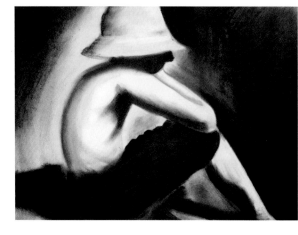

Black and white tonal painting by Alice Watanabe (child artist).

Norham Castle, Sunrise, 1845. Turner fills this landscape with a magical, hazy light.

Toulouse-Lautrec, Henri de

(1864-1901)

Toulouse-Lautrec was a French painter who is most famous for his posters and for being very short! (He was about five feet tall but had an unusually large head.) He loved to paint the seedy side of Paris night life and lived wildly, dying young at the age of 36. He was influenced by Japanese **prints** and his theatre posters used large, flat, bold shapes and strong colours. His were the first posters that were taken seriously as works of art.

trompe-l'oeil

Trompe-l'oeil is a French phrase which means 'deceive the eye'. It is used to describe pictures that are deliberately intended to make viewers believe that what they see is real and not just a painted illusion.

Turner, J. M. W.

(1775-1851)

Joseph Mallord William Turner was a British painter whose **landscapes** were painted in a wild and free way that was very unusual at the time when they were painted. He loved to show extremes of weather such as blizzards and rough seas. Not everyone liked Turner's work at the time – a critic described one of his stormy seascapes as 'soapsuds and whitewash' – but his paintings have been popular and admired for more than 100 years.

U V

Uccello, Paolo

(1397-1475)

Paolo Uccello was an Italian painter who specialized in showing **perspective** in his work. At the time perspective was a newly discovered technique, and he set himself difficult perspective problems to see if he could overcome them. His paintings have other strong qualities of **design** and **composition** too.

 Battle of San Romano, c.1450. Beneath the hooves of the charging horses, Uccello uses the fallen knight and the broken lances to show his skill with perspective.

Velázquez, Diego

(1599-1660)

Velázquez was a Spanish artist who became the court painter to King Philip IV. He is most famous for the natural life and character in his work – very unlike the formal **portraits** of so many other court painters. Whether he painted a dwarf (kept for the King's amusement) or the Pope, he approached them with the same observant eye.

Vermeer, Jan

(1632-75)

The Dutch painter Jan Vermeer was an absolute master of the simple domestic scene where one or two figures are captured in a simple task, such as playing a musical instrument or preparing food. Vermeer turned these straightforward pictures into masterpieces of light, colour and human feeling. His work did not make him famous during his lifetime and he struggled to earn enough money to feed his fifteen children.

▷ The Painter in his Studio, 1665. A fascinating glimpse of Vermeer at work.

Veronese, Paolo

(1528-88)

Veronese was an Italian painter from Venice, living around the same time as **Titian**. He loved to paint large scenes, filled with people. He was especially known for his pictures of biblical feasts, but he got into trouble for crowding too many people into his painting of the Last Supper. People demanded to know why there was a servant with a nosebleed, a man carrying a parrot, several dwarfs and other extras. Veronese got round this problem by changing the name of the painting to 'The Feast in the House of Levi'!

Vuillard, Edouard

(1868-1940)

Edouard Vuillard, the French painter, was a friend and colleague of **Bonnard** and, like him, painted moody interiors often featuring his family and groups of his friends.

W

Wallis, Alfred

(1855-1942)
Alfred Wallis was the best known of all British **naive** painters. A retired Cornish fisherman, he started painting to relieve his loneliness after the death of his wife. He painted sailing ships and **landscapes** in ship's paint on any scrap of wood or cardboard that he could find. Though the **perspective** of his paintings is technically 'wrong', they have vibrant energy and a flavour of the Cornish coast.

war artist

During World War I and II, the British government commissioned artists to paint their experiences of battle. **Stanley Spencer** and **Graham Sutherland** are some of the best-known official war artists.

Warhol, Andy

(1928-87)
Andy Warhol was the most famous of the American pop artists. He became well known in the 1960s for his repeated images of soup cans, Coke bottles and the actress Marilyn Monroe. He rebelled against the idea of art as a unique, hand-made piece of work. He called his studio 'the factory' and had many assistants to help him print his work. He had a talent for publicity and became a famous star in his own lifetime, appearing regularly in the newspapers and gossip pages. He also made unusual films. One of his films simply showed a shot of the Empire State Building for eight hours. Warhol said, 'I like boring things'. When he died his estate was worth an estimated $100 million.

Watteau, Jean-Antoine

(1684-1721)
Watteau was a French painter who specialized in light, romantic scenes in parkland settings, filled with beautifully dressed young people who seemed to be without a care in the world.

 Marilyn diptych, 1962. Andy Warhol chose to use Marilyn Monroe's face over and over again, because it was a symbol of pop glamour.

Y

Whistler, James Abbott McNeill

(1834-1903)
Whistler was born in America but spent most of his working life in England. He was influenced by the **impressionists** and was determined that people should see his paintings just as paintings and not think that they had any special meaning. He gave them titles such as 'nocturne' or 'symphony' as if they were pieces of music. For example the famous picture known as 'Whistler's Mother' was named 'Arrangement in Grey and Black'. He was a loud man who managed to annoy and upset a lot of people during his lifetime.

Whiteread, Rachel

(1963-)
Rachel Whiteread is a living British artist who casts large objects in concrete. She is interested in making us look at spaces that people do not always notice – like the space underneath a chair. In 1994 she won the Turner Prize, a British art award, for a work called 'House' in which she filled the middle of a London terrace house with concrete, and peeled the walls away. The result looked like a house but also like a tomb. Although people in the art world wanted this work to be kept, it was destroyed by the local council shortly after it was finished.

Wood, Grant

(1892-1942)
Grant Wood was an American painter from Iowa. He is known for one painting, 'American Gothic', a pin-sharp picture of a traditional farming couple in front of their house. It has become an image of the hardworking people of middle America, repeated in books and on postcards all over the world.

Wyeth, Andrew

(1917-)
Andrew Wyeth paints pictures that remind people of America in the past, showing wooden buildings and rusting farm machinery, beautifully painted and tinged with sadness. Like **Grant Wood** he is also famous for one picture, 'Christina's World'. This picture has become one of the best-known images in American art.

△ *Christina's World, 1948. Christina Olson, a disabled friend of Andrew Wyeth, looks up towards her house at the top of an empty hill.*

Yeats, Jack Butler

(1871-1957)
Jack Yeats was an Irish painter and brother of the poet W. B. Yeats. He began work as an illustrator and in his early years as a painter was inspired by the **impressionists**. He went on to develop his own lively, loose and colourful style similar to the work of his friend, the Austrian painter **Oskar Kokoschka**. Yeats believed strongly that Ireland should be an independent country and his paintings were mostly of scenes from Celtic mythology and everyday Irish life. He was also a poet, novelist and playwright.